I0502553

The Bridal Guide to

Wedding Photography

This book is dedicated to my wonderful wife Kathy,
that I share my life with, my sole mate, my best friend and
my everything! Thank you for being you!

-Craig

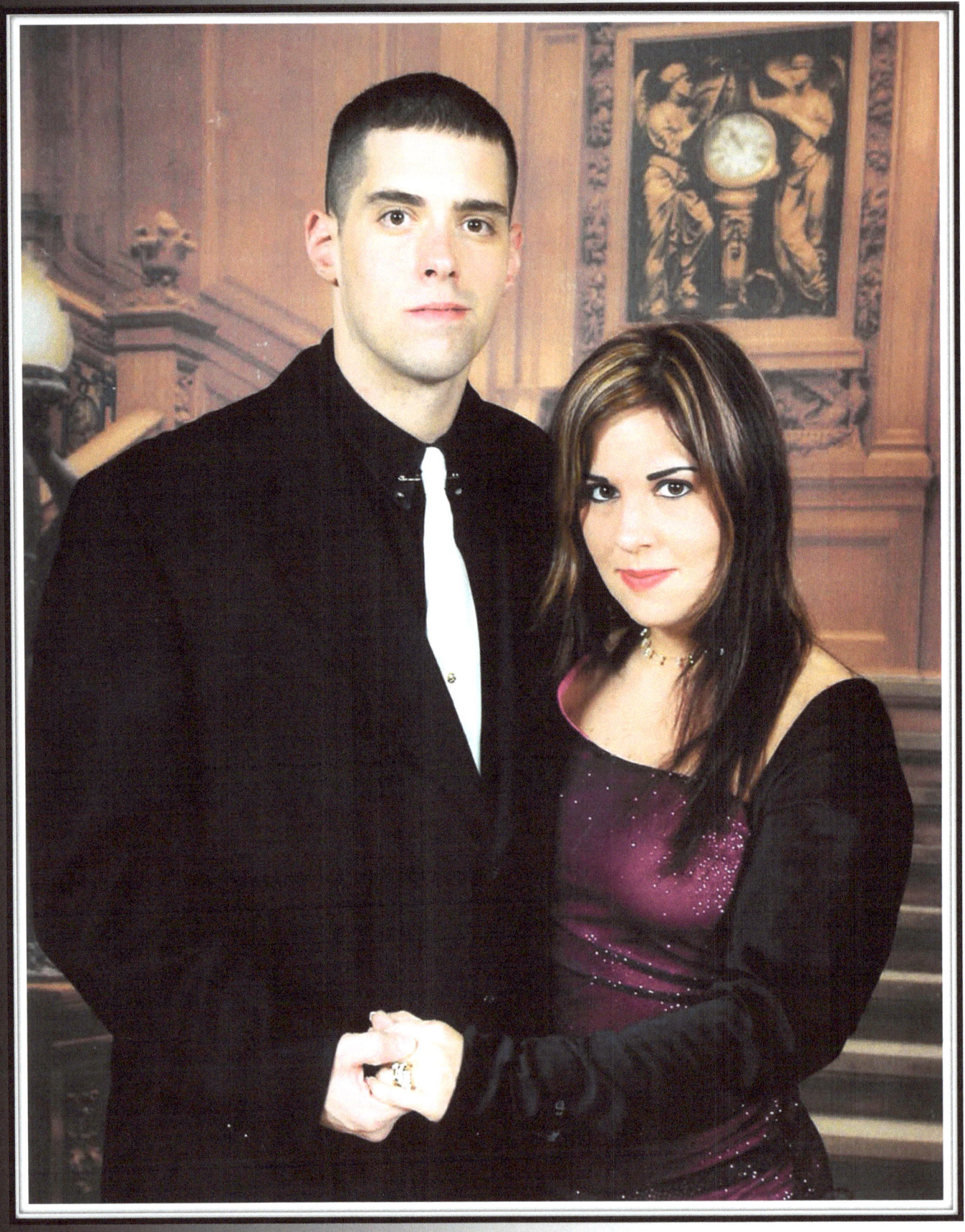

Craig & Kathy Pardini

The Bridal Guide to

Wedding Photography

Author:

Craig A. Pardini, M.P.R., A.C.E.

Editor:

Kathy L. Ireland Pardini

Photographs by:

Pardini Photography and Weddings

www.pardiniphotography.com

240.426.0098

© 2013 Pardini Photography and Weddings

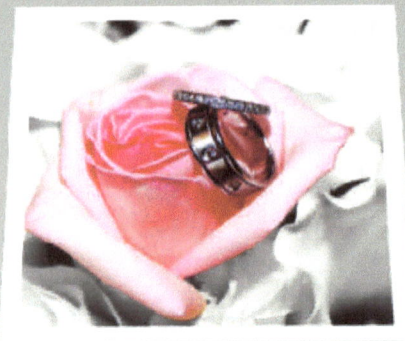

Months after the wedding, memories fade and the night is forgotten. When all is said and done, the photographer is the only vendor that is delivering a product that is designed with the future in mind.

Photography, the best way to tell stories

Introduction

He got on one knee and popped the question and you said, "YES!" or maybe it was the other way around. But any-way...you are engaged and will soon be married!

First and foremost—Congratulations!

At this point, the ball is rolling….your family and friends are told and everyone you know hears the exciting news, "it's time for a wedding"!

While many of your friends will only have to bring a special dress or suit out of the closet, you have a lot of work ahead of you and there is a wedding to plan for! The photographer has one of the most important jobs that is involved with your wedding. After the wedding is over, "Precious memories fade in our minds uncontrollably, sometimes....we can't help it....it happens to all of us" - *(Kathy Ireland-Pardini)* and only the photographs are left to tell a story of the most important day of your lives!

It is our job to make the photography piece of your wedding as easy as possible and give you breathtaking photographs that will document the most memorable event in your life.   We are taking the time to compose this book "The Bridal Guide to Wedding Photography" to help make your wedding as smooth as possible and to give you advance tips to make your wedding day picturesque and to give you helpful posing techniques.

It all starts with you

What kind of photographs do you want on your wedding day? We already know your answer: "breathtaking ones!" Although this is a good and true answer, there is much more than that....

Determine your personal taste and interest:

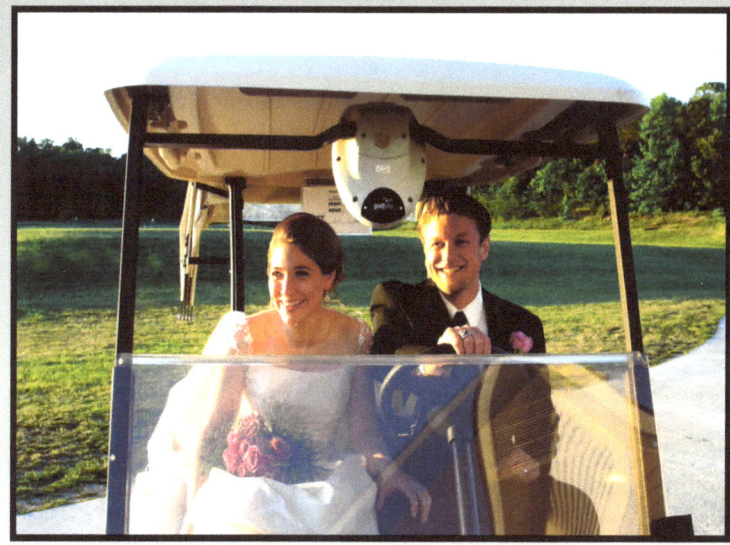

1. Will your ceremony be in a traditional church or another type of venue?

2. Will there be a bridal party and how many?

3. Are you wearing a wedding gown with a long, medium or no train? Headpiece? Veil?

4. Do you plan on being walked down the aisle by your dad, both parents, or are you going alone or with someone else?

5. How close is your family? Do you want a photograph with each one of your siblings? How large do you want to go in our extended family formal photographs?

6. Do you plan in arranging the day so that there is a specific time allowed for posed formal portraits?

7. At the reception, do you want the DJ to announce your grand entrance, first dance, the toast, the cake cutting and any other special events?

8. Do you want to throw your bouquet? Will the groom toss the garter?

9. Do you want the garter catcher to put the garter on the bouquet catcher?

10. Will any part of your wedding take place outdoors or in very low lighted room?

There are many different photo opportunities during your wedding and the more your photographer knows in advance, the more preparation they will have, which will help ensure that they capture the most important events of your wedding.

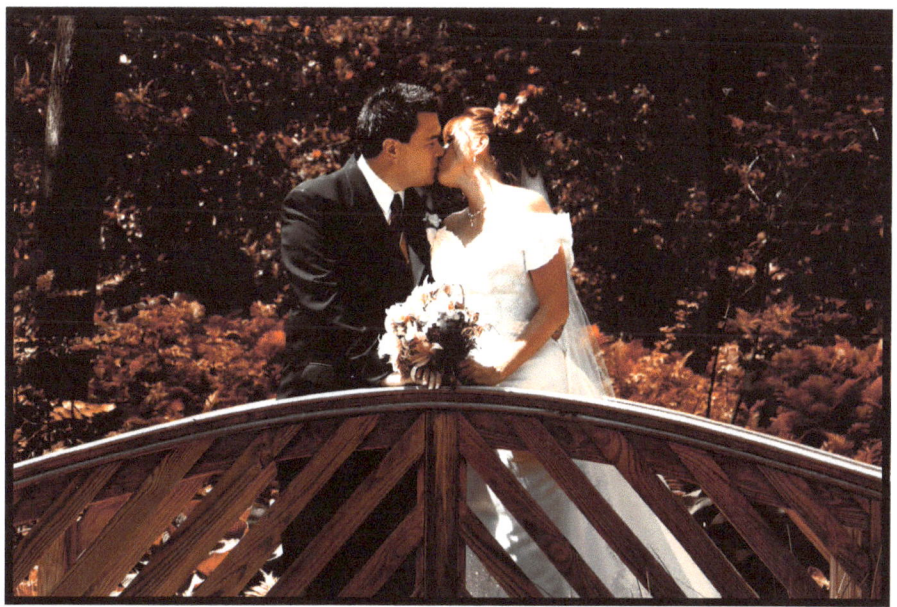

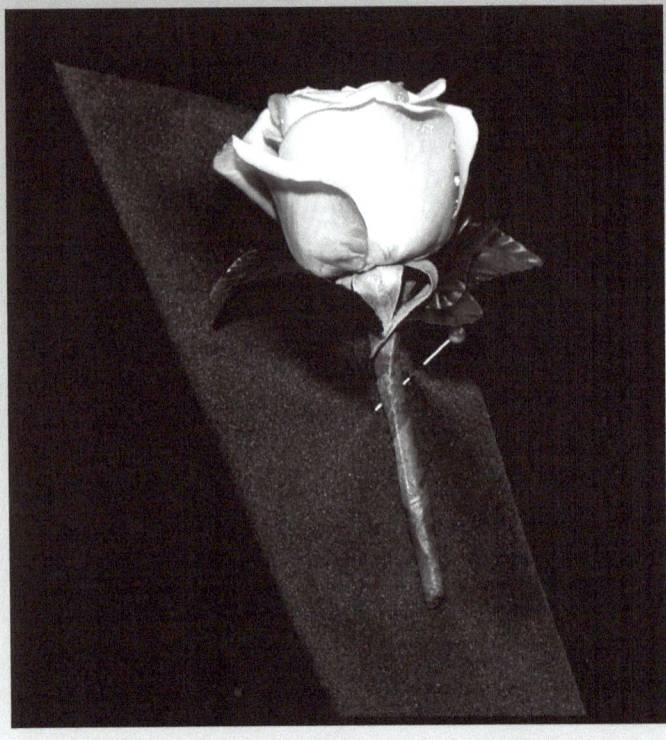

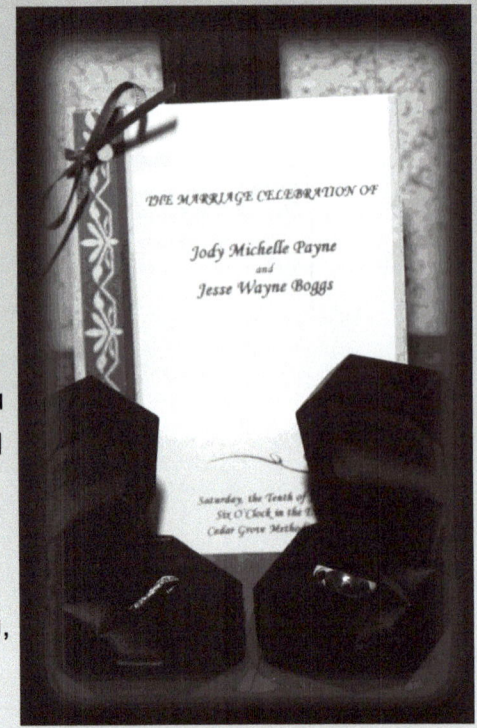

Accessories and other items used in the wedding make a great photograph to help you remember all the small details of your special day. If there are any items that have a special meaning to you, make sure you let us know so we can capture it! Please do not assume we will know that you want pictures of your class ring, tools of the trade or dad's cuf-flinks.

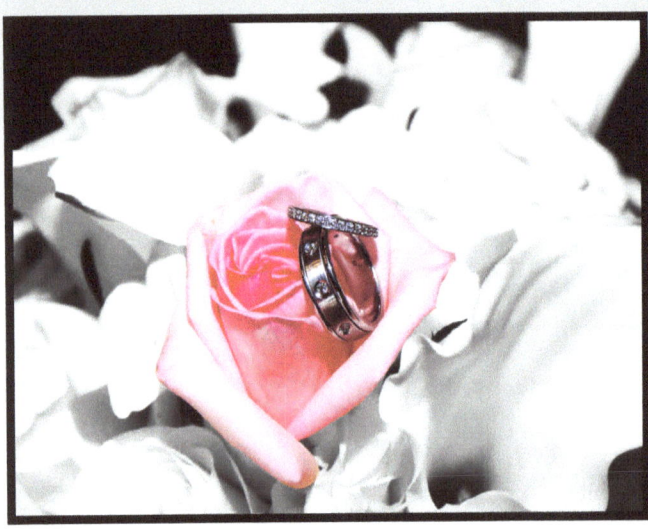

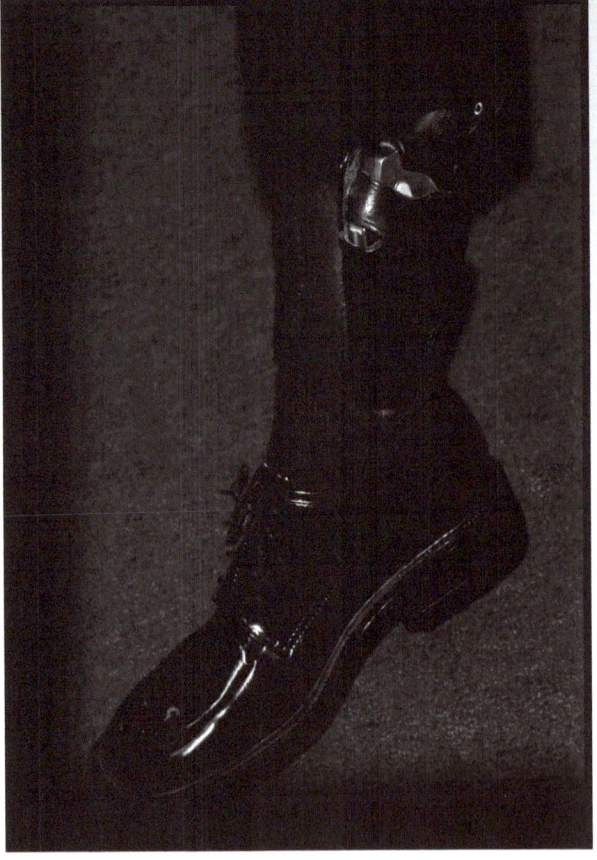

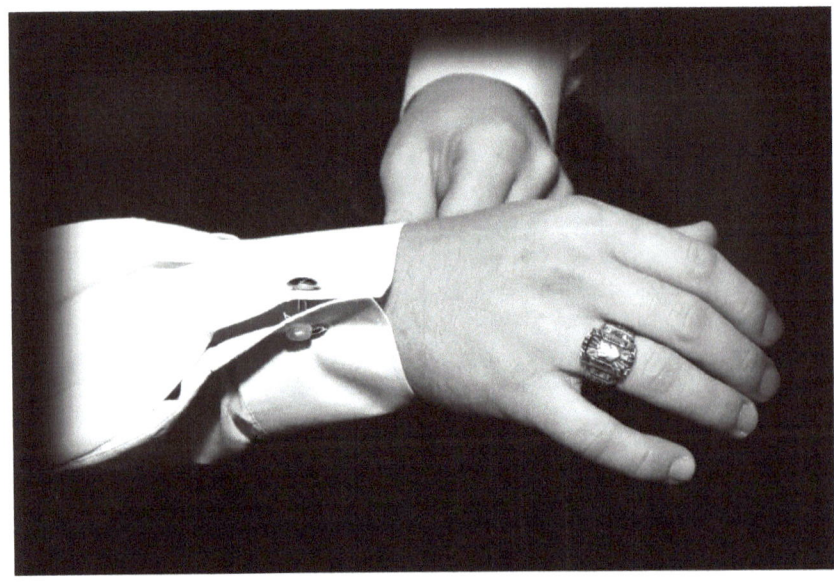

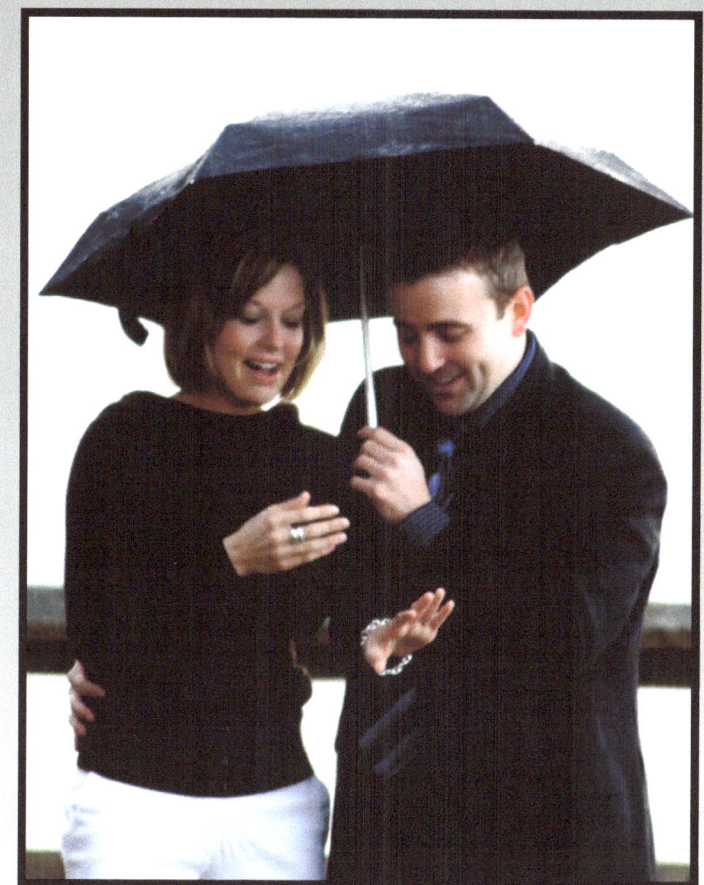
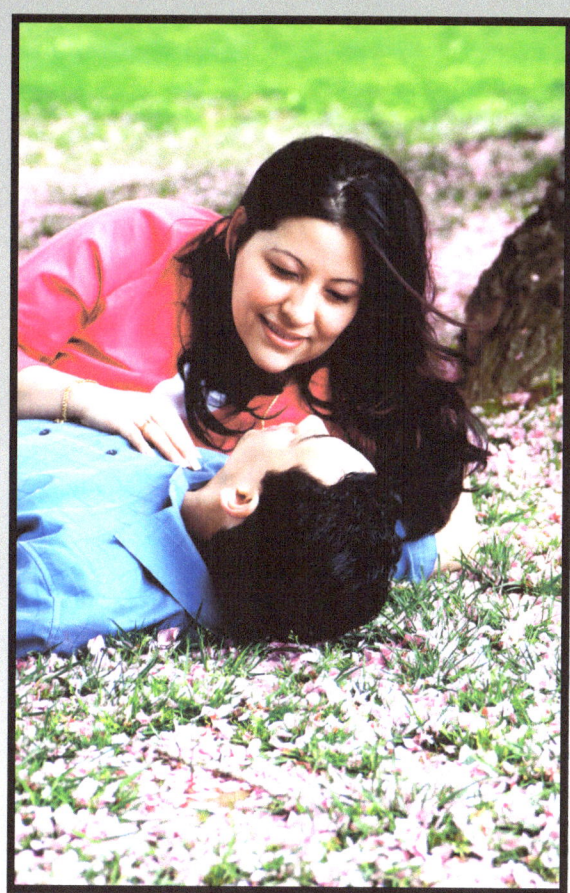

Besides your wedding photographs, it is also nice to have engagement photographs. Engagement photographs are nice to give out to family members and friends in holiday cards, wedding invitations and to display at the actual wedding for guests to sign and write notes around the board-er. We offer an engagement photograph session complementary with all wedding packages.

Engagement photo sessions are a great way for the photographers and the couple to know each other so during the big day, there is more of a friendship relationship than a client / vendor relationship.

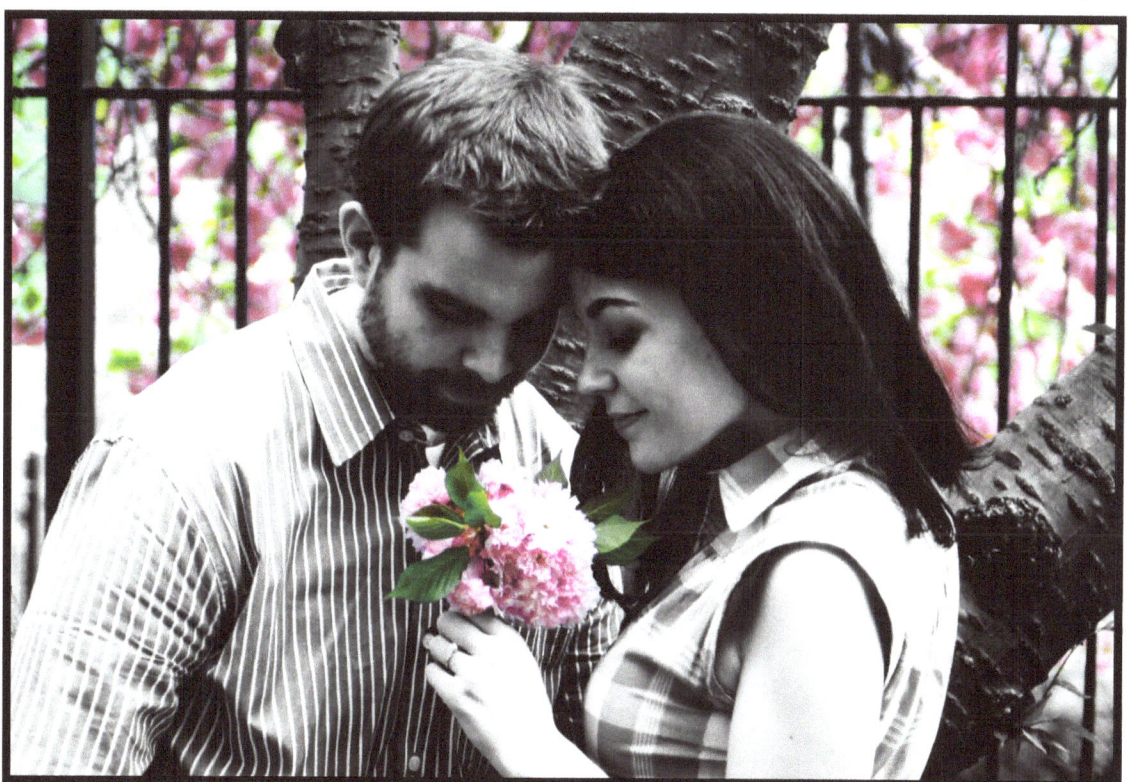

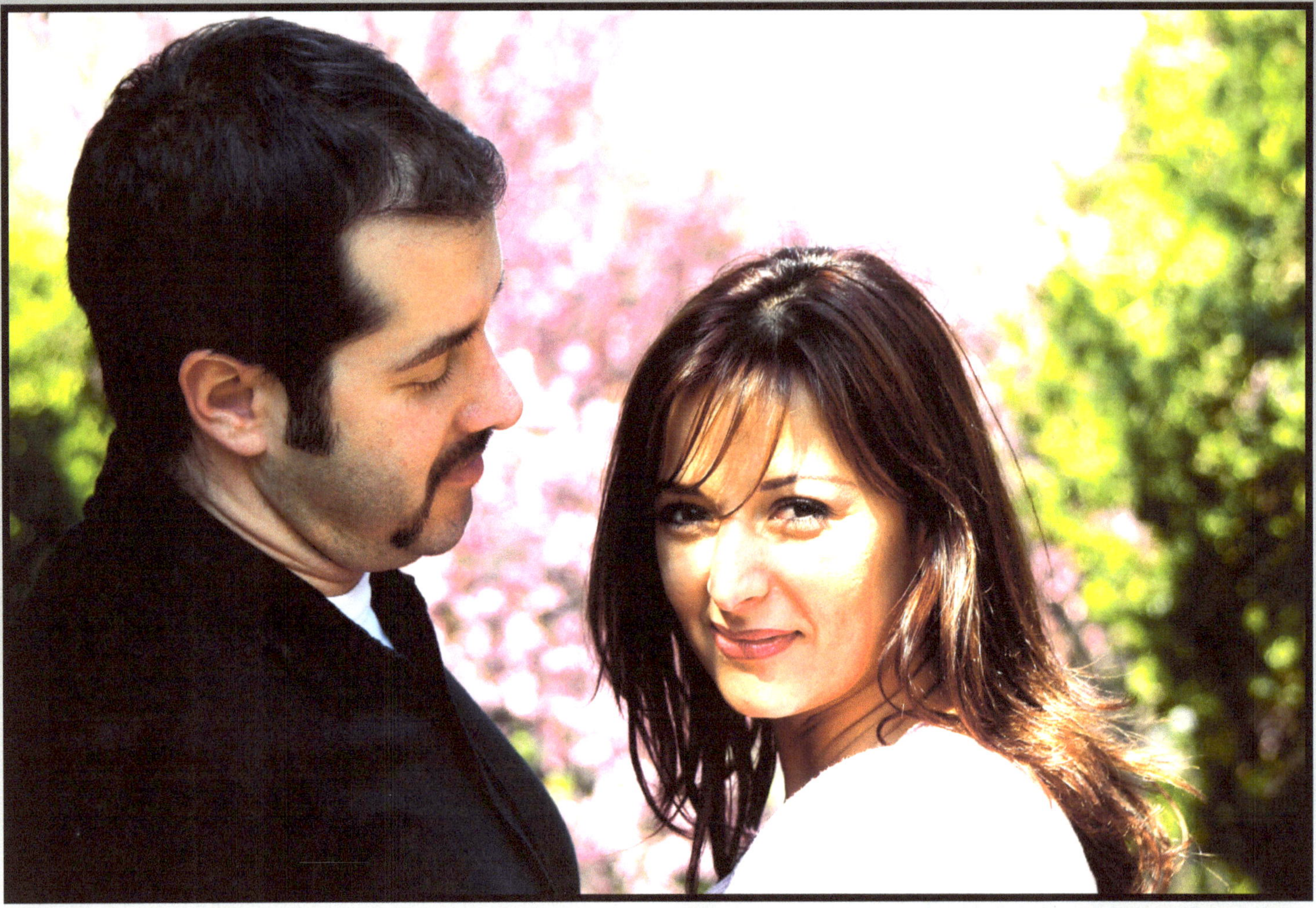

A picturesque background makes for a work of art! When you plan your wedding, it is a good idea to pick a date when flowers are in bloom if you are looking for a lot of color in your backgrounds. We try to reserve April and May for our outdoor engagement photo sessions for this reason.....

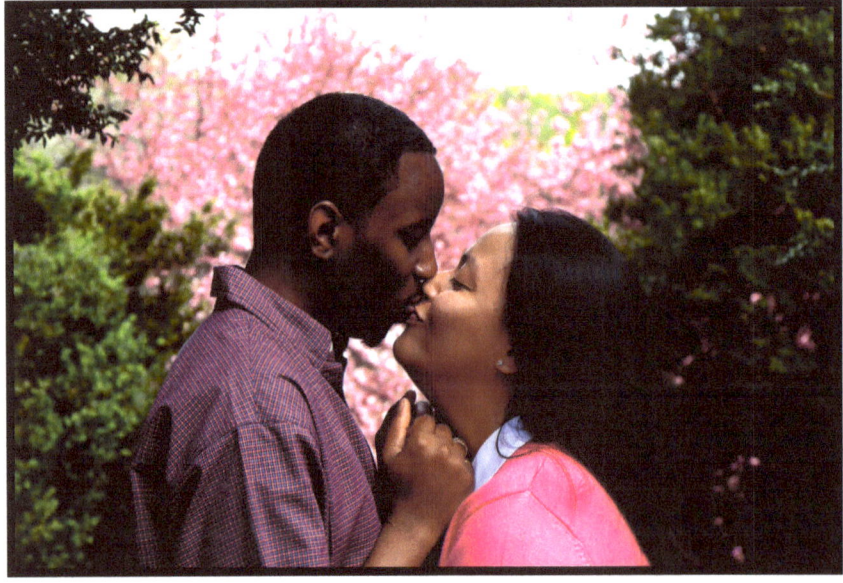

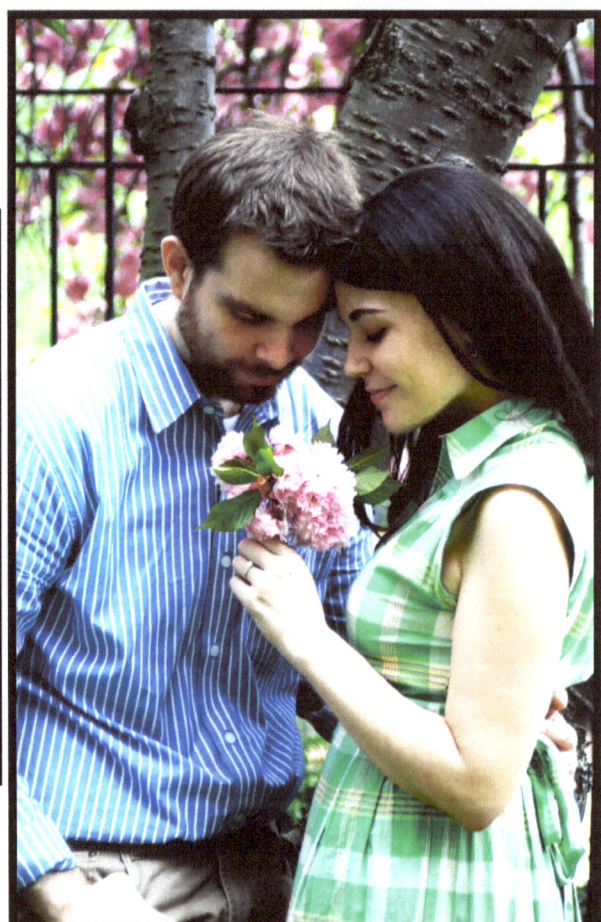

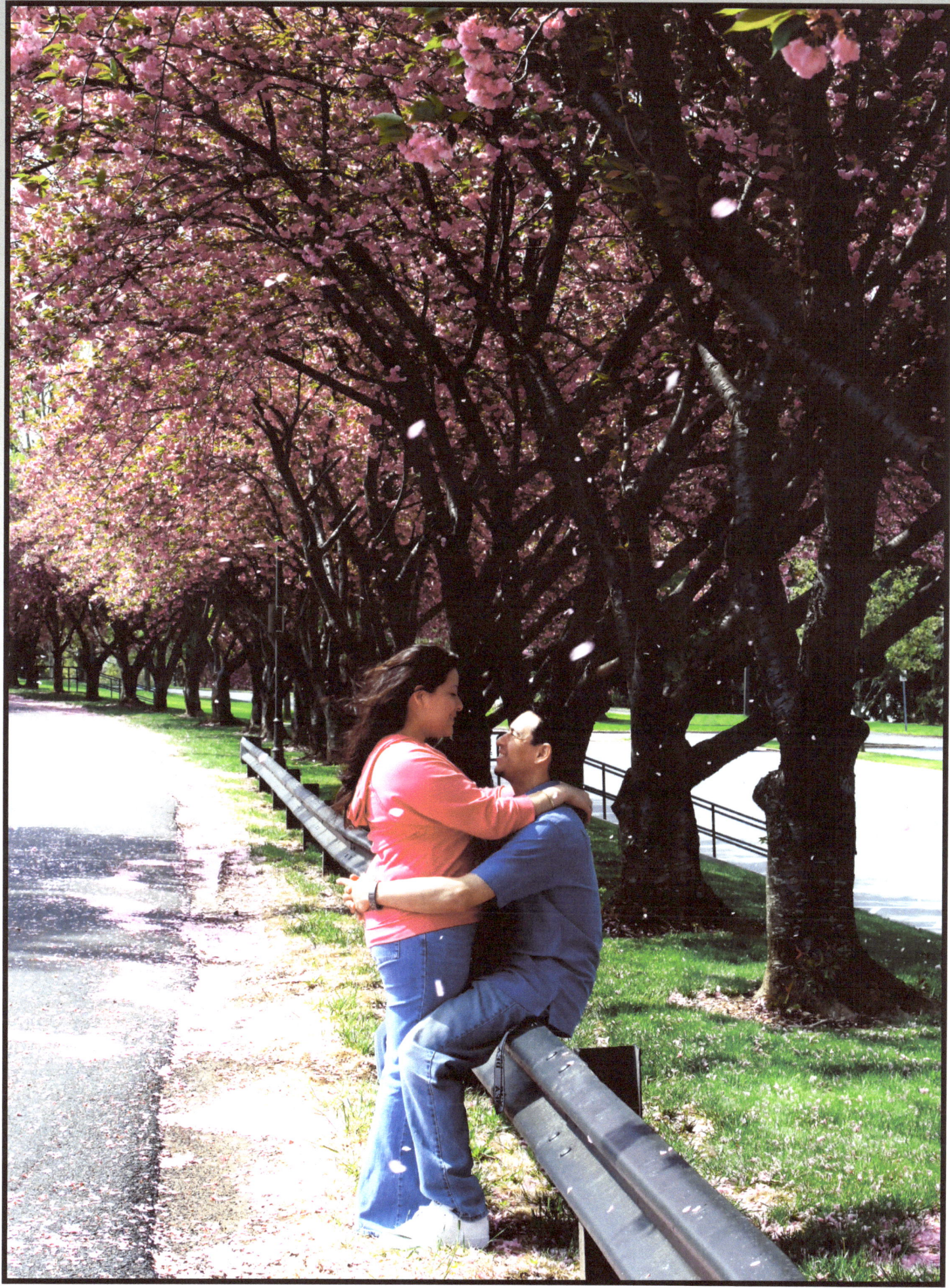

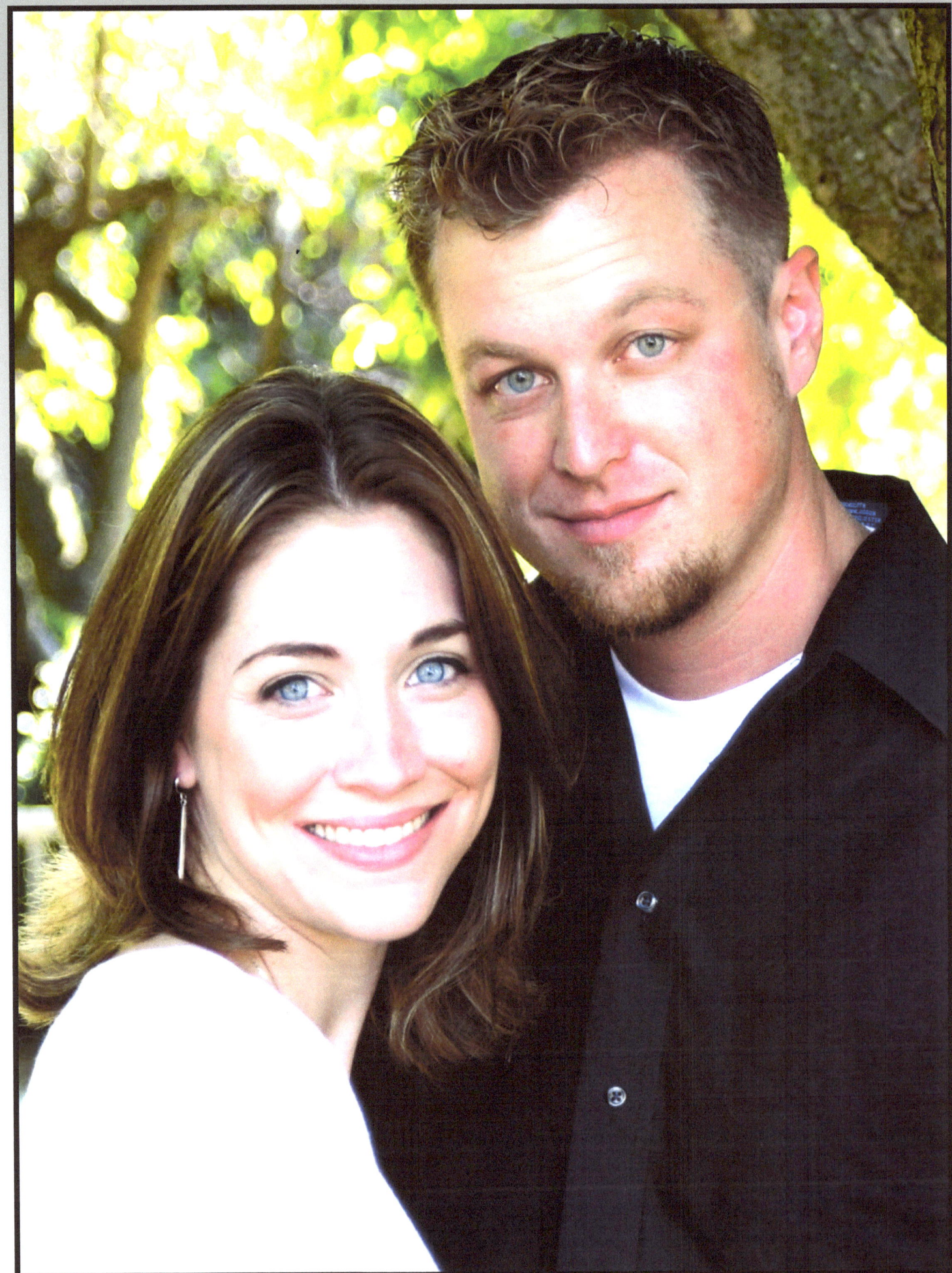

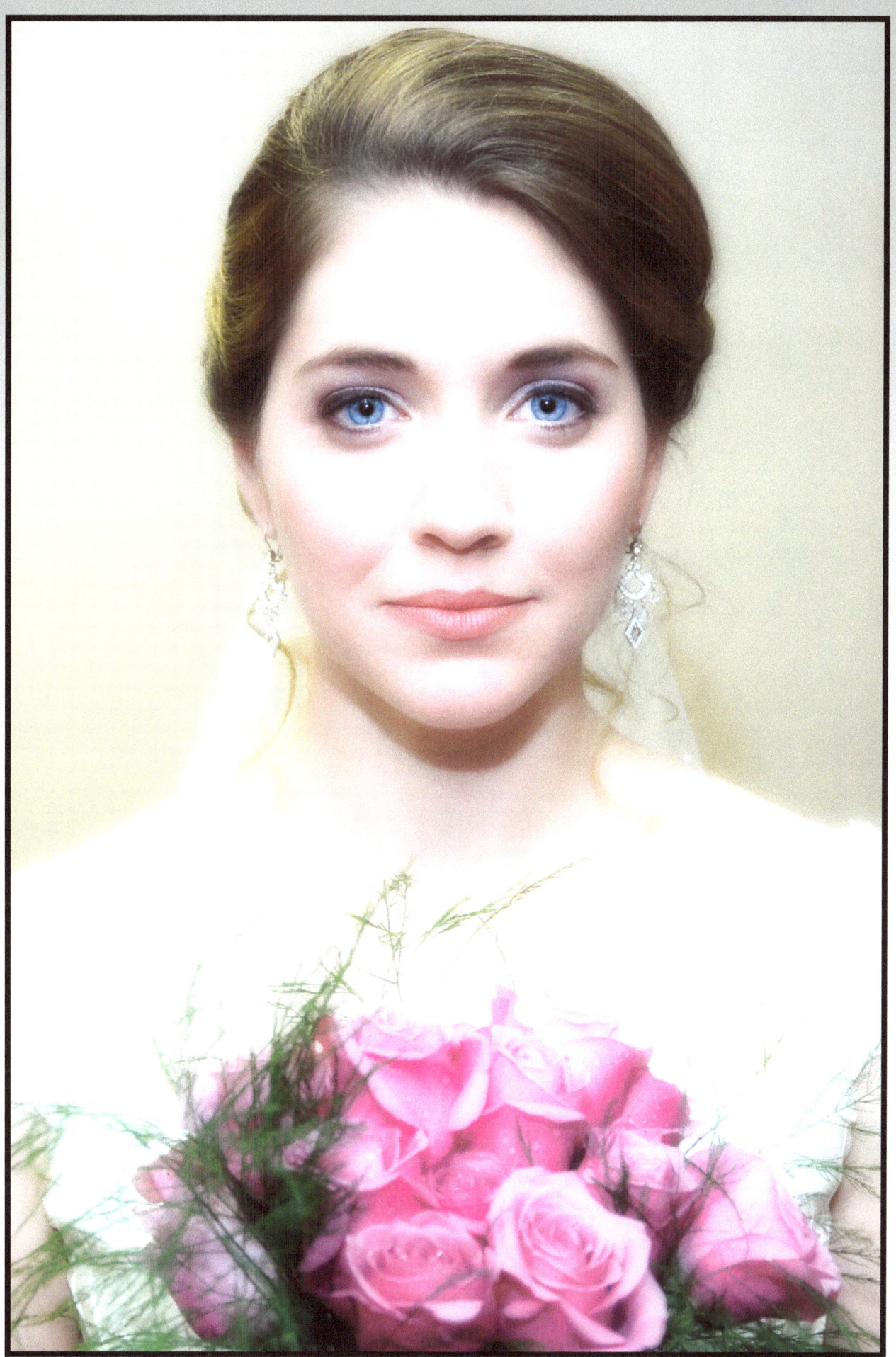

One of the hardest decisions you will have to make is determining who to trust to document your special day for a lifetime. With today's technology, most searches are done on the internet. You can almost determine how creative and

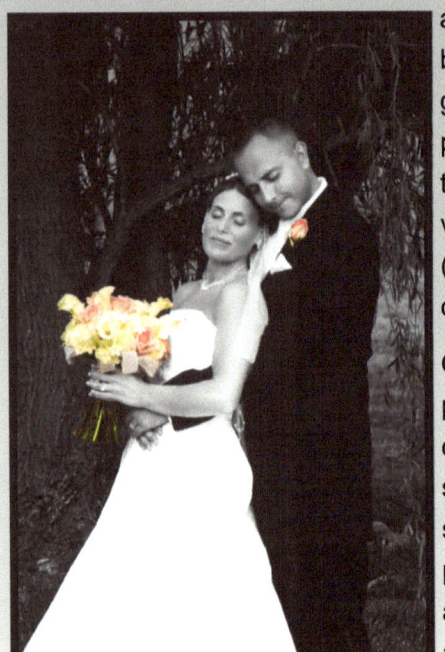

artistic a photographer is by their website. If you see a very elegant website with beautiful photographs, you can tell that the photographer is artistic and there is a good chance that your photographs will look the same. If you see a website that is pieced together and looks pretty bad, you can almost bet, your photographs will look the same. But be careful: some photographers have professional webmasters develop their websites for them. That is why we take pride in our website (www.pardiniphotography.com). We also design and maintain our website on our own!

One thing you may have noticed during your search is almost every photographer has different prices and packages. We took the liberty of visiting many different websites to learn what types of packages and prices are out there and to see what the others are doing wrong. You can see price ranging from $500 to $15,000, depending on the experience of the photographer and packages offered. Remember, you don't always get what you pay for…. our basic pack-

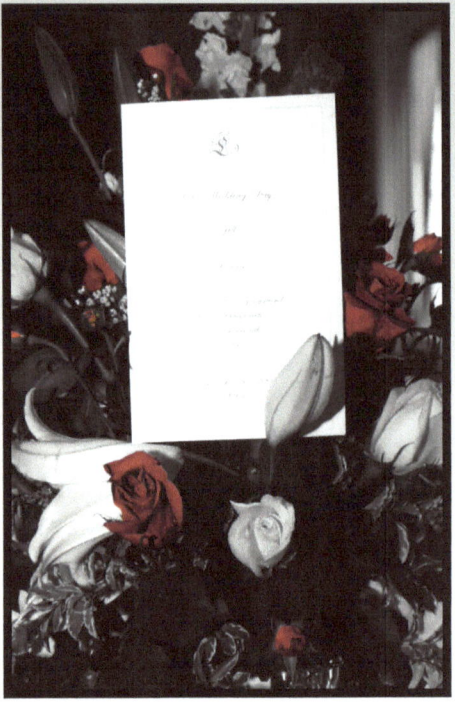

age is in the $2,000 range. Pricing isn't everything, so be careful with who you choose….just because the package is $10,000, doesn't mean that your are getting a great photographer. We enjoy what we do and feel that pricing should not be too high. One of the reasons we charge less is because we don't take wedding photographs for a living, we do it because we are good at it and enjoy it! One of the advantages of hiring us, is that we will be timely - arriving at your wedding promptly, and getting the results to you on time. We have the right equipment for photographing your wedding. Having photographed many weddings in our career, we will be at ease at your wedding, and are experienced in working with individuals, couples, and groups to make the formal photography go smoothly. When you think about the cost of photography, remember that you, your parents, your extended family and your friends will be **investing time** with us during your wedding. Don't waste time on your wedding day with a photographer who won't produce results you will love!

How do you select what package is right for our wedding? Once you know what your wedding will consist of; how

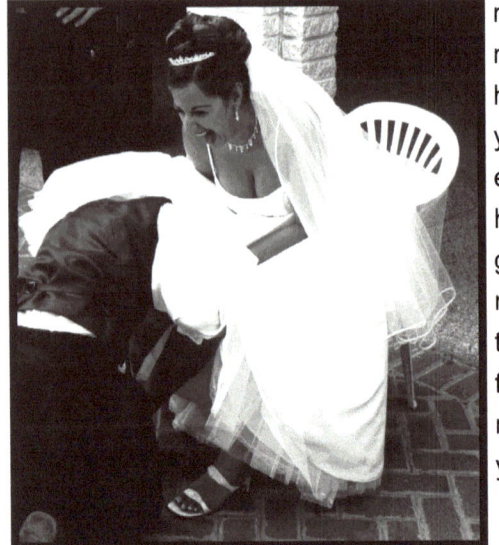

many guests, locations and the length of the day, you will want to figure out how many hours you will need photo coverage for. Please, please, please, do not have a friend or family member that has photography as a side hobby capture your special once in a lifetime moments. If you are spending the time and money to have the best day of your life, you will want to make the investment on having a professional cover the entire day: bride and party getting dressed, groom and guys getting ready, pre ceremony moments, ceremony, posed formal photographs and reception until the end. This is the only time in your life that this will happen and you will regret not having this documented by pictures for a lifetime so you can view the day anytime you feel like it and share your moments with family and friends that could not make it. This is the only time that you will have a day like this, so do it right!

Photographs taken during the day

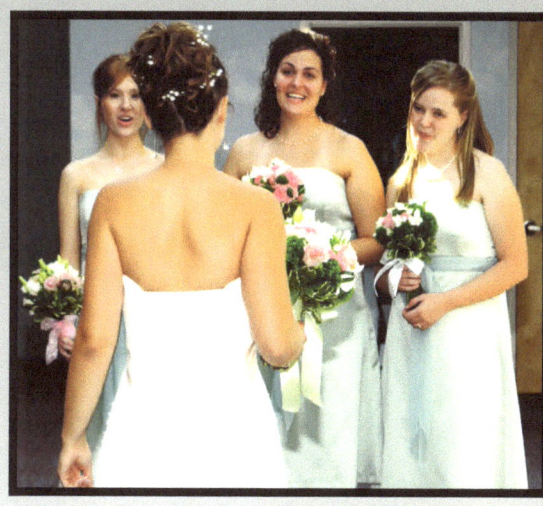

These are just a few important moments that will be captured throughout the day and there will be several different poses of the shots below ....

Pre-Ceremony

- ☐ Bride having hair done
- ☐ Bride doing makeup
- ☐ Bride looking in mirror
- ☐ Bride with her girls (group and single)
- ☐ Bride with her parents (both and single)
- ☐ Bride with other family members
- ☐ Groom getting ready
- ☐ Boutonnieres being put on
- ☐ Groom with his guys (group and single)
- ☐ Groom with his parents (both and single)
- ☐ Groom with other family members
- ☐ The bridal bouquet and flowers
- ☐ The rings
- ☐ The wedding program / invitation
- ☐ Guest book
- ☐ The church / venue (shots throughout)
- ☐ Other candid shots

The Ceremony

- ☐ Family being escorted down
- ☐ Groom and his guys entering and lining up
- ☐ Bridesmaids walking down the aisle
- ☐ Matron or maid of honor walking down the aisle

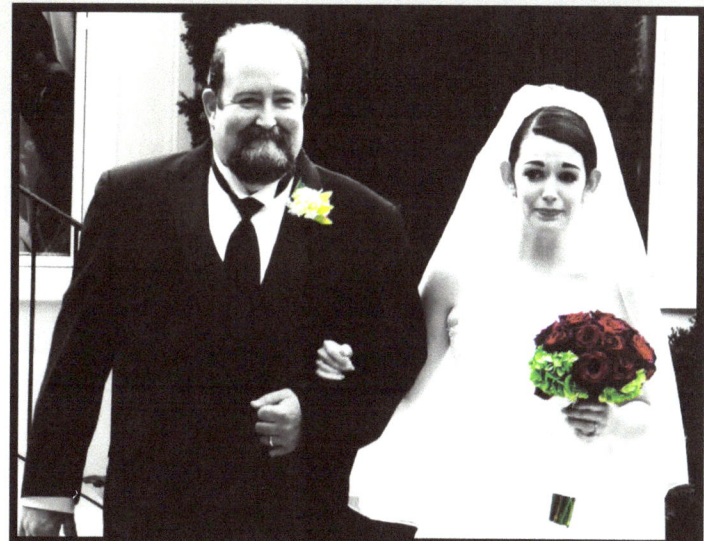

- ☐ Flower girls and ring bearer walking down the aisle
- ☐ Bride and dad walking down the aisle
- ☐ Dad kissing bride and removing veil
- ☐ Dad handing over the bride
- ☐ Many shots throughout the ceremony and traditions

After the Vows

- ☐ The recessional
- ☐ Receiving line
- ☐ Leaving the church
- ☐ Getting into the limousine or getaway car

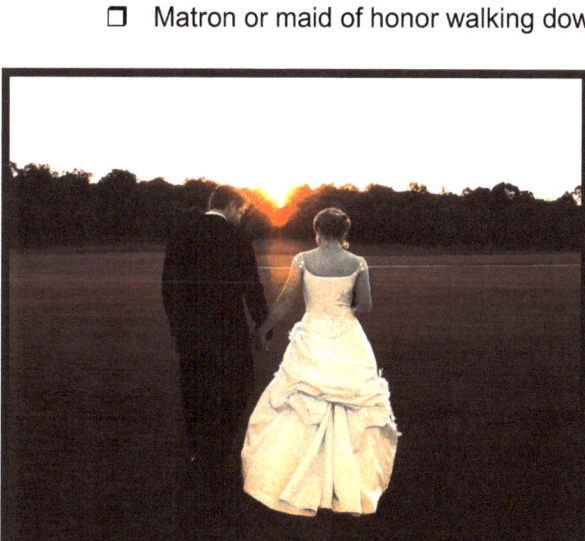

Posed formal photographs

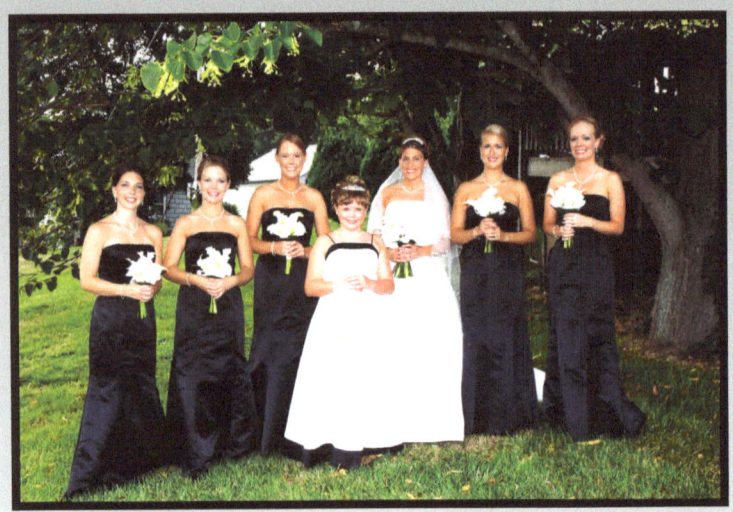

Between the time of the interview/1st meeting and the time of the wedding, we would like to communicate frequently (email or a quick telephone conversation) and spend time together during an engagement photography session. This will put both you and us at ease during the wedding. We enjoy hearing how the plans are going and the special details, like dress and flower colors. We are as excited as you are and we want to hear all the news! It is also a good idea to have a conference call a day or two before the wedding to finalize the details! One of the details that you will need to think of is the family members and close friends that you would like to have photographs taken of during the posed formal photographs. A general rule of thumb is to allow at least 45 minutes for the posed formal photographs and usually immediately take place after the ceremony and prior to the reception. We have photographed many different weddings and photographed some that only allowed 10 minutes for these photos and many important photographs were missed. We have created a list to give you assistance in thinking what photos you would like to have. We recommend that you review the general formal pose list prior to your wedding to ensure all is covered and add or delete any that is applicable to your special day. Normally, during the posed formal photographs, it is recommended that you assign a family member or the wedding coordinator to assist us in identifying and calling up your family and friends for the photographs. This will help speed things up, help run smoothly and most of all to ensure no one is missed. Below is a sample list of average photographs taken during the posed formal photographs. In each pose, there will be multiple angles, close-ups and full lengths. We will also take 3-4 photographs of the same pose to ensure everyone's eyes are open, looking the same direction, etc.

Family

- ❏ Bride and groom with officiator
- ❏ Bride and groom with all of the Bride's family (as big as the bride would like to go)
- ❏ Bride and groom with brides immediate family
- ❏ Bride and groom with bride's parents
- ❏ Bride with her parents
- ❏ Bride with her mother
- ❏ Bride with her father (straight, kissing cheek)
- ❏ Bride and groom with all of the groom's family (as big as the bride would like to go)
- ❏ Bride and groom with groom's immediate family
- ❏ Bride and groom with groom's parents
- ❏ Groom with his parents
- ❏ Groom with his mother (straight, kissing cheek)
- ❏ Groom with his father
- ❏ Bride and groom with both sets of parents
- ❏ Any other family shots w/ bride and groom (e.g. favorite uncle, best friend, generations photograph, etc.)

Wedding Party

❒ Bride and groom with bridal party standing (straight and u-shape)

❒ Bride and groom with bridal party sitting (chairs or men kneeling and bridesmaids sitting on their knees)

❒ Bride and groom with bridal party (alternating male and female)

❒ Bride with bridesmaids (all, each alone)

❒ Bride and groomsmen

❒ Groom with groomsmen (all, each alone)

❒ Groom with bridesmaids

Bride and Groom

❒ Bride and groom looking forward full length, ¾, and very close-up (several different angles)

❒ Groom looking at bride while bride looks forward, full length, ¾, and very close-up

❒ Bride looking at groom while groom looks forward, full length, ¾, and very close-up

❒ Bride and groom with foreheads touching, eyes closed, full length, ¾, and very close-up

❒ Groom kissing bride at the altar, full length, ¾, and very close-up (lips and cheeks)

❒ Groom kissing bride at the altar tight head shot pose (lips and cheeks)

❒ Groom putting ring on bride's finger

❒ Bride putting ring on groom's finger

❒ Bride and groom lighting candles, full length, ¾, and very close-up

❒ Bride and groom's hands with rings over flowers and bride with ring over flowers

❒ Rings over flowers (alone)

❒ Other missed shots during ceremony

Bride

❒ Looking straight

❒ Smelling flowers

❒ Flowers around bottom of dress

❒ Shoes

❒ Torso holding flowers, neck down

Groom

❒ Looking straight

❒ Hands in pockets

❒ Cufflinks

❒ Torso with tie and flower, neck down

❒ Shoes

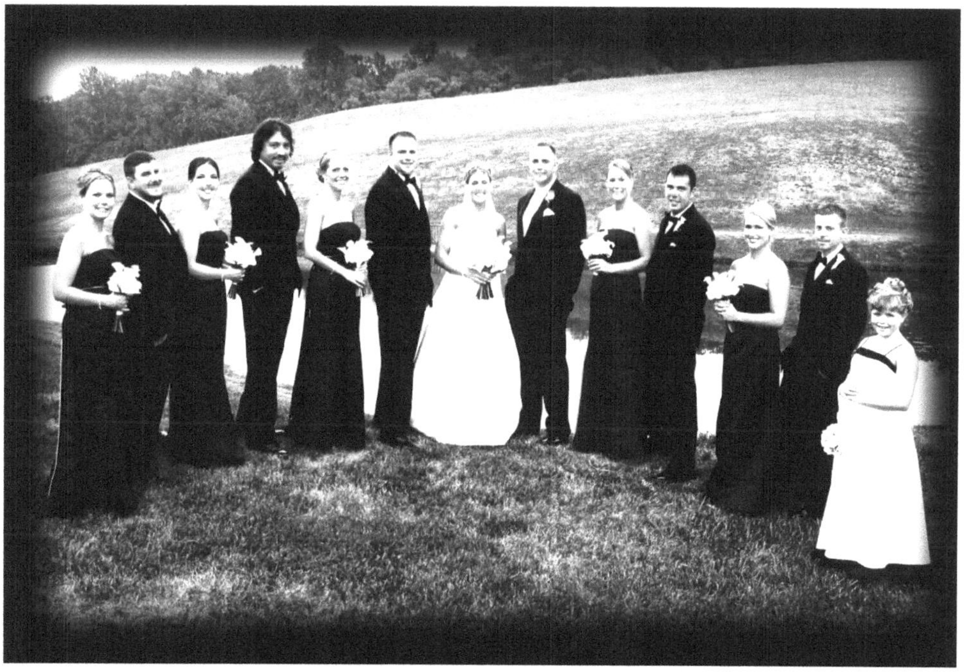

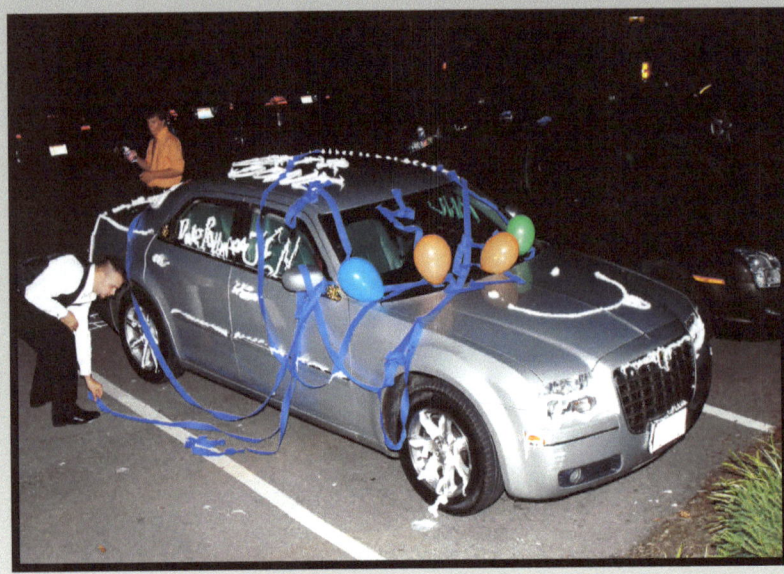

The Reception

- ❏ Different shots around the venue
- ❏ Cake
- ❏ Tables with decorations
- ❏ The entrance
- ❏ The first dance
- ❏ The toast
- ❏ The food
- ❏ Table shots of guests
- ❏ Candid's of guests dancing and talking
- ❏ Groups of guests on the dance floor
- ❏ Special dances
- ❏ Romantic shots (candles, available light night scenery)
- ❏ The cake
- ❏ Bouquet and garter toss
- ❏ Family traditions

This is an example of a low lighted night scene that makes a nice romantic moment

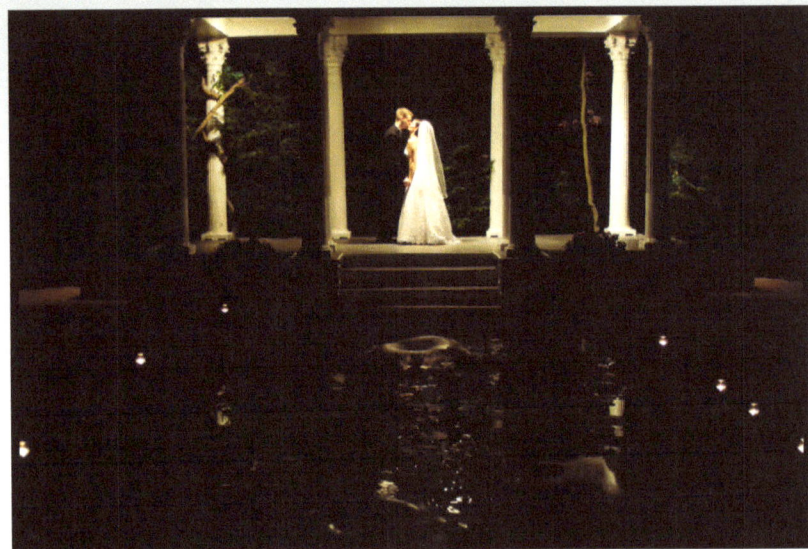

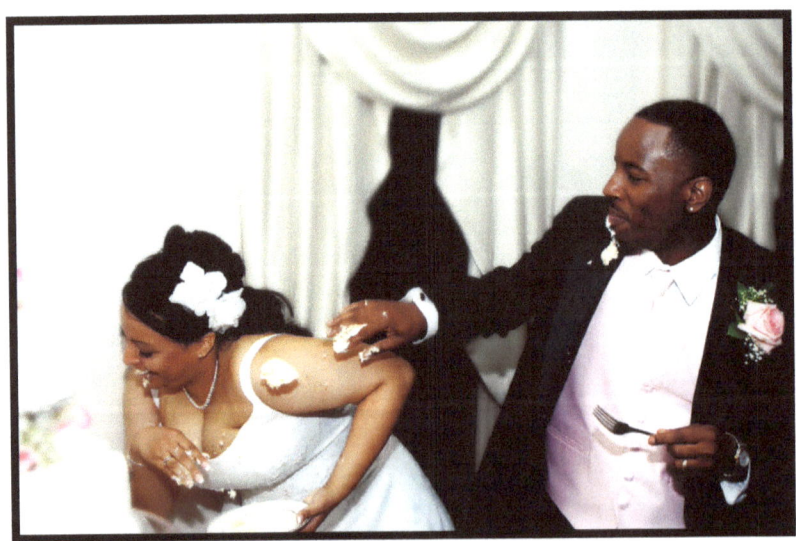

Please be nice to each other when feeding the cake. We have seen some brides put a little cake on the grooms nose and the groom turns around nails the bride with cake. Although, this does make for an excellent shot!

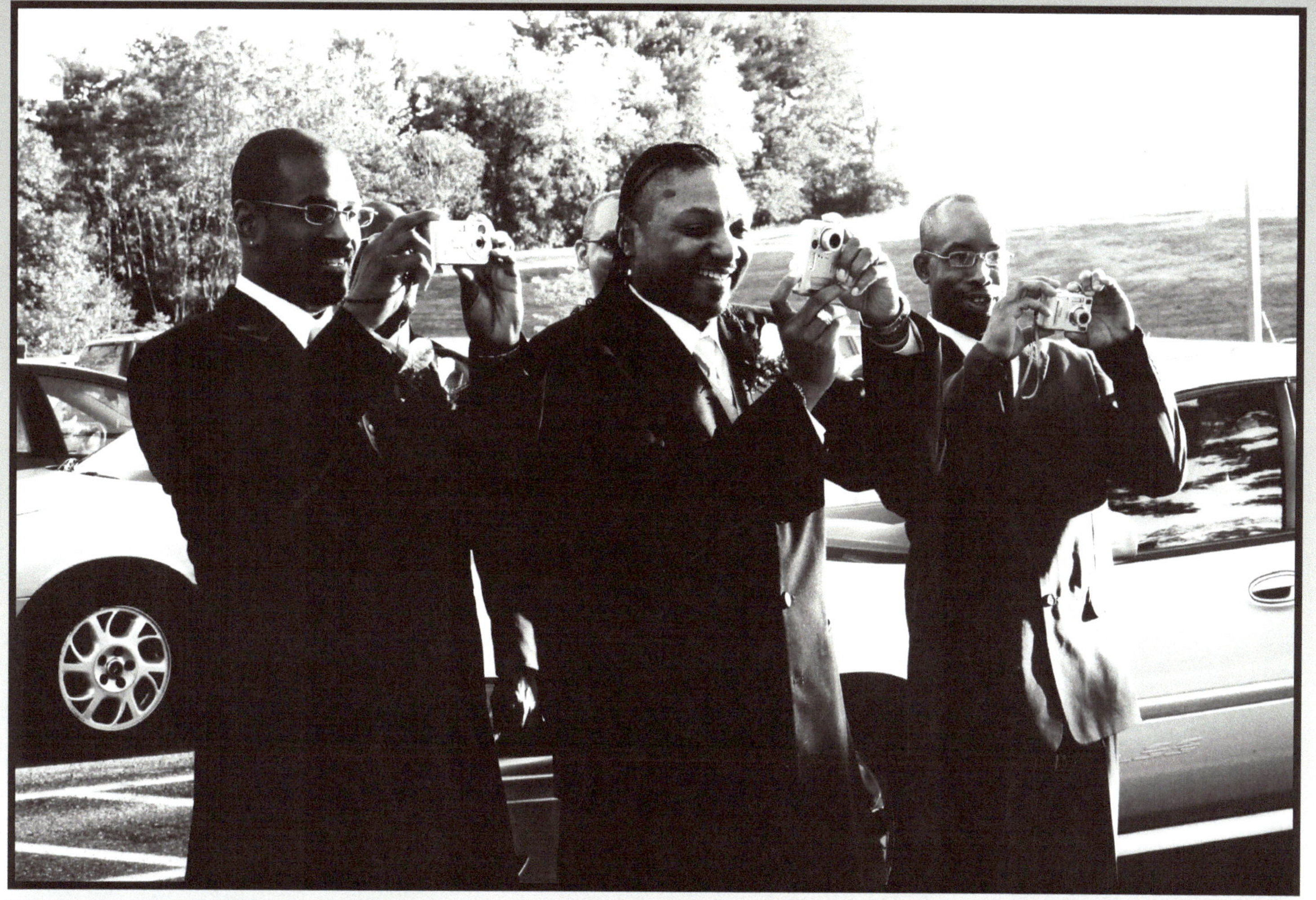

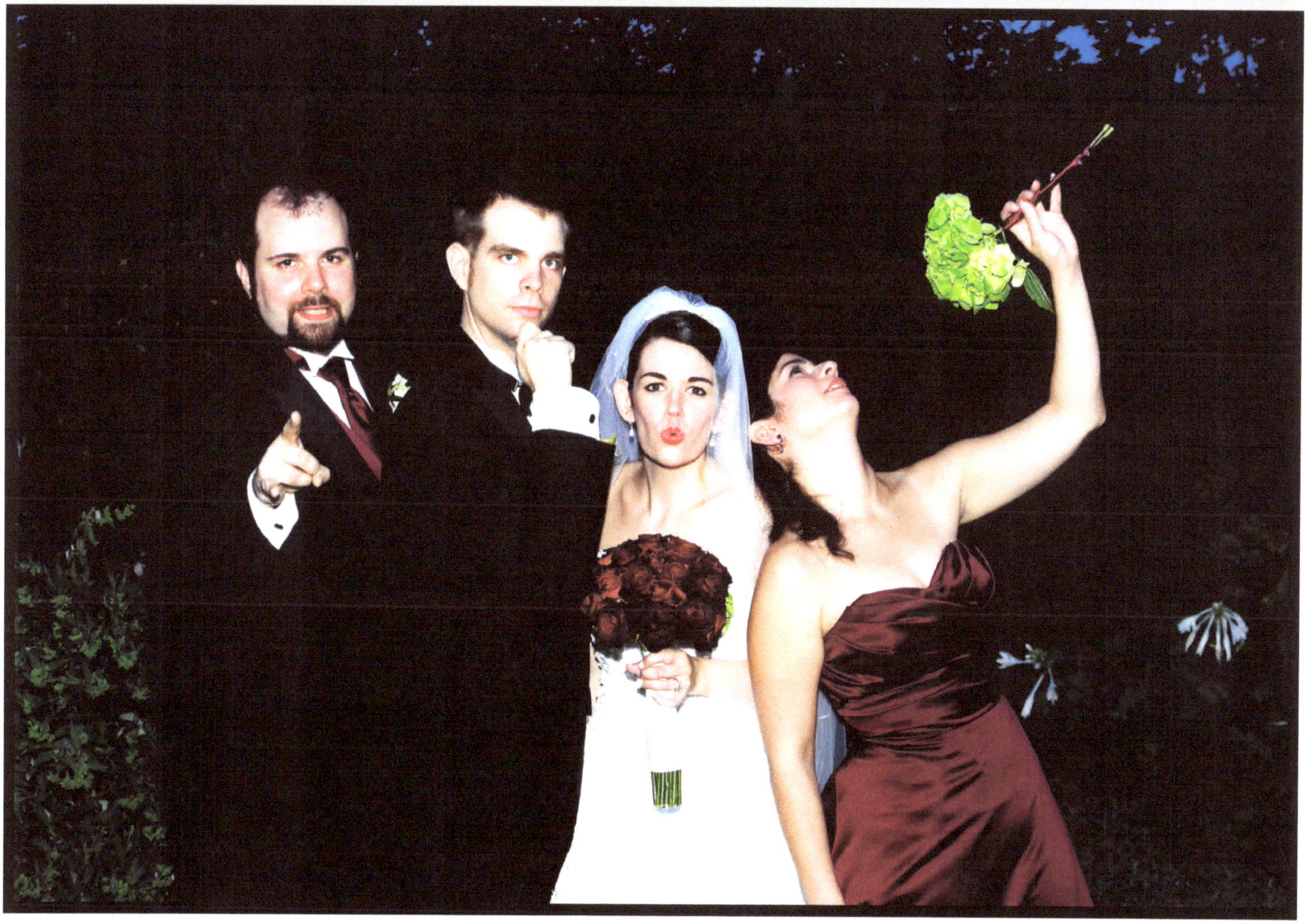

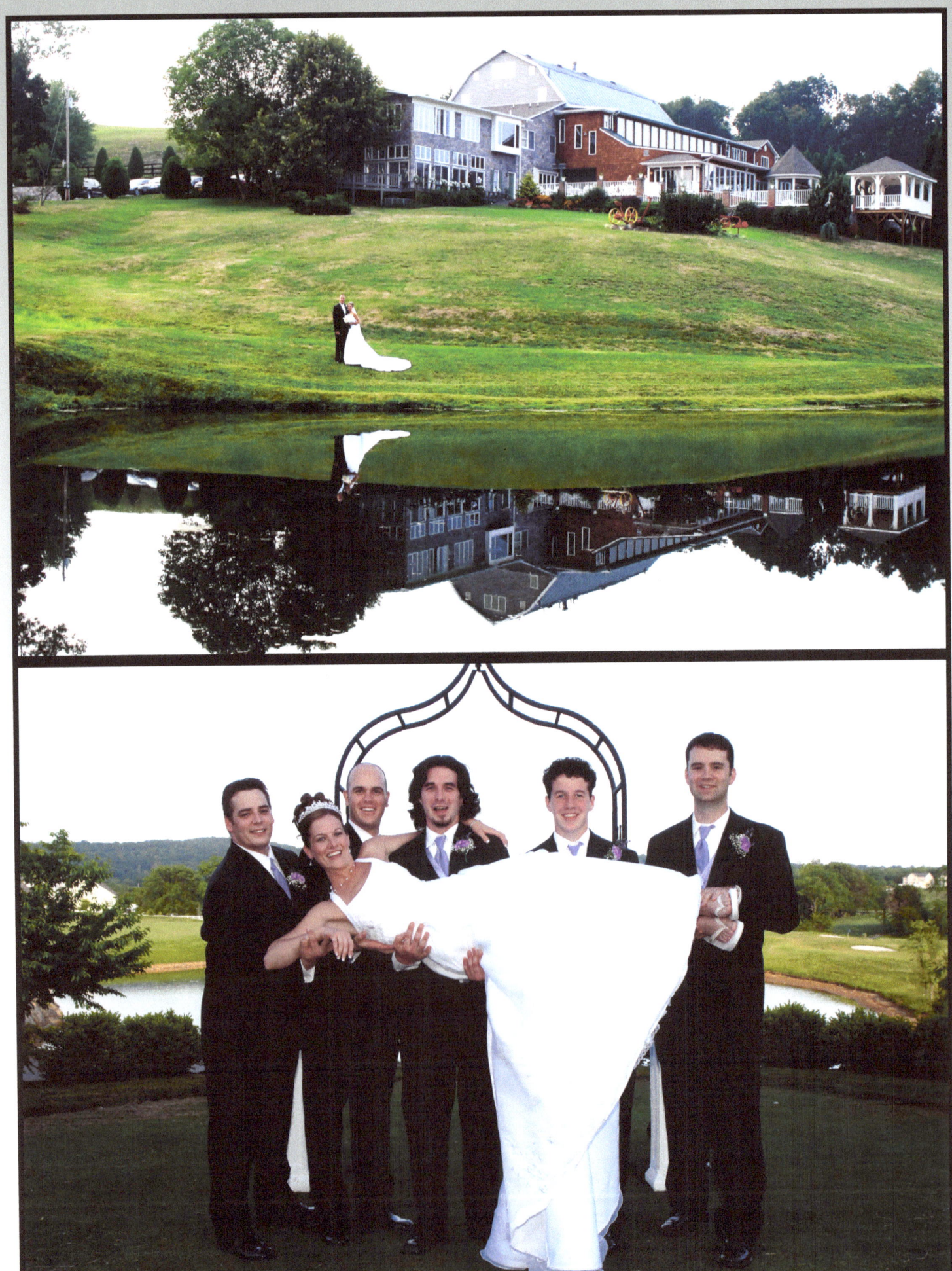

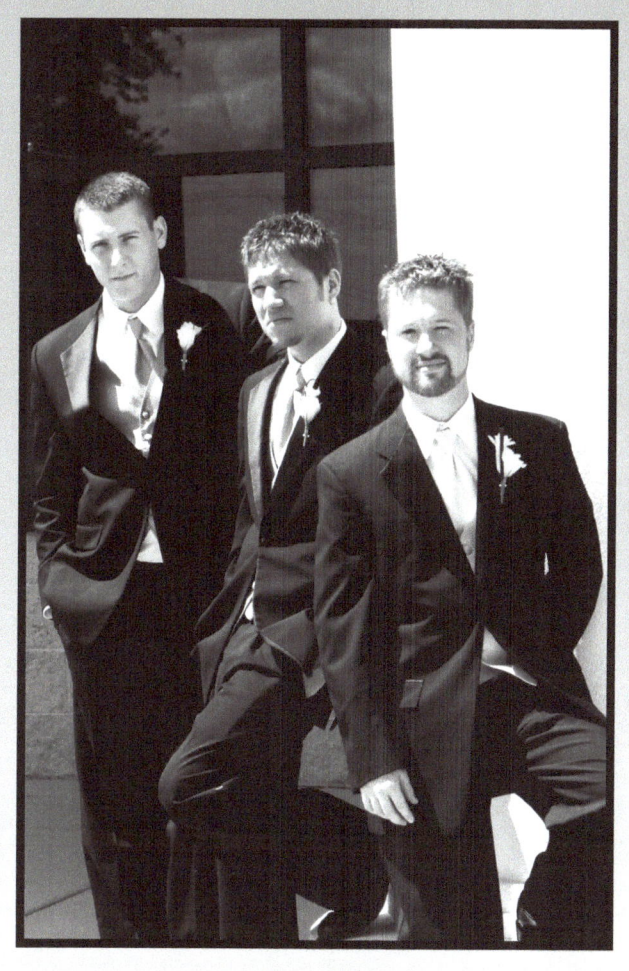

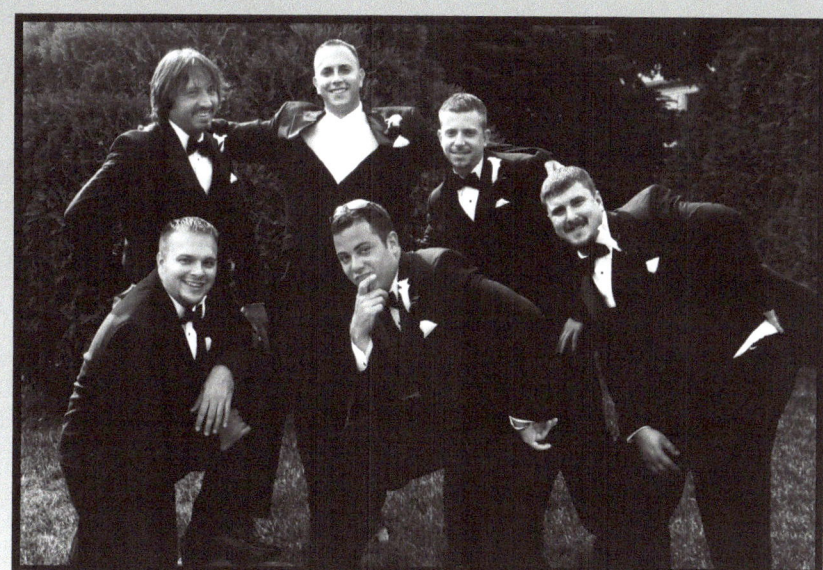

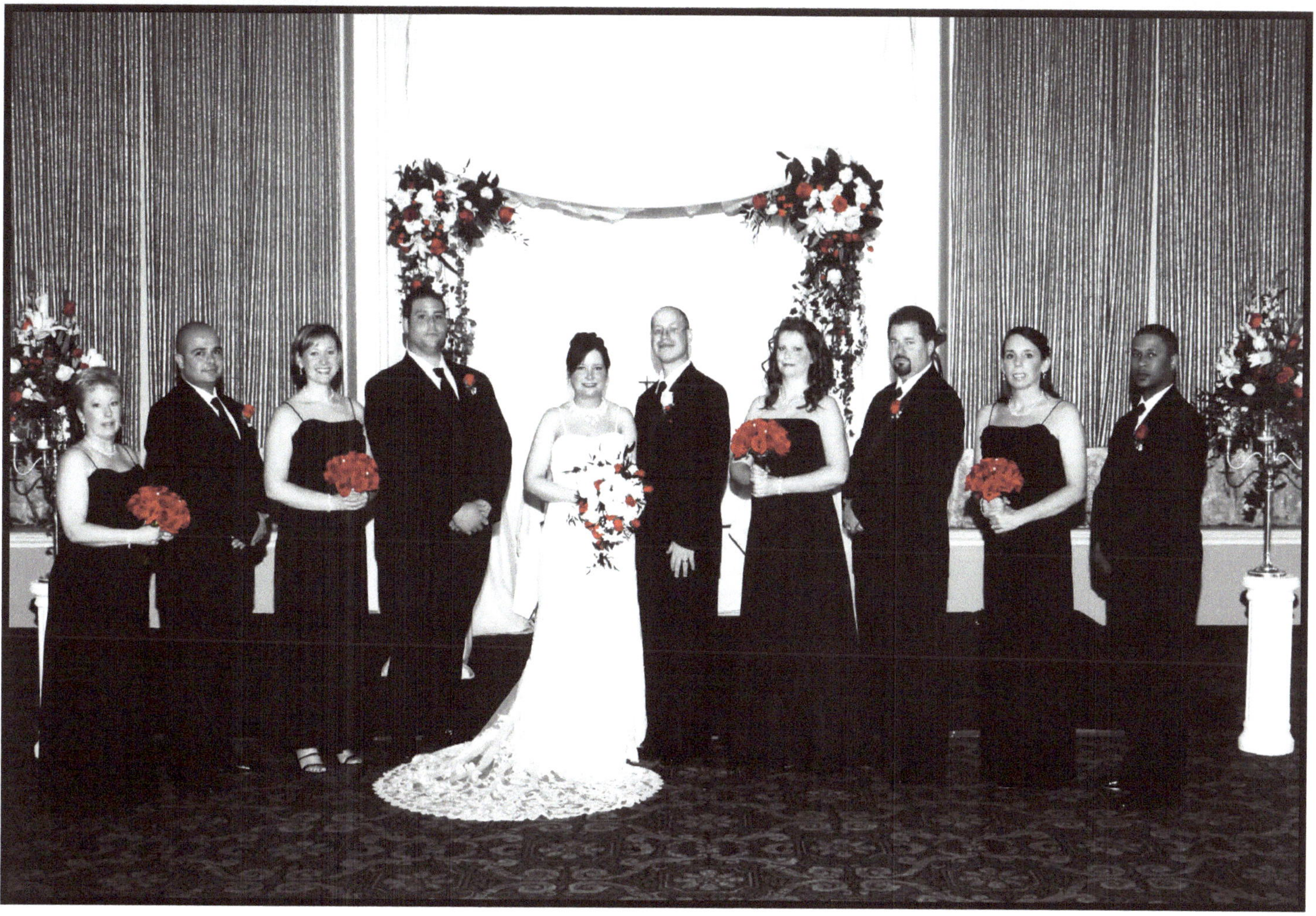

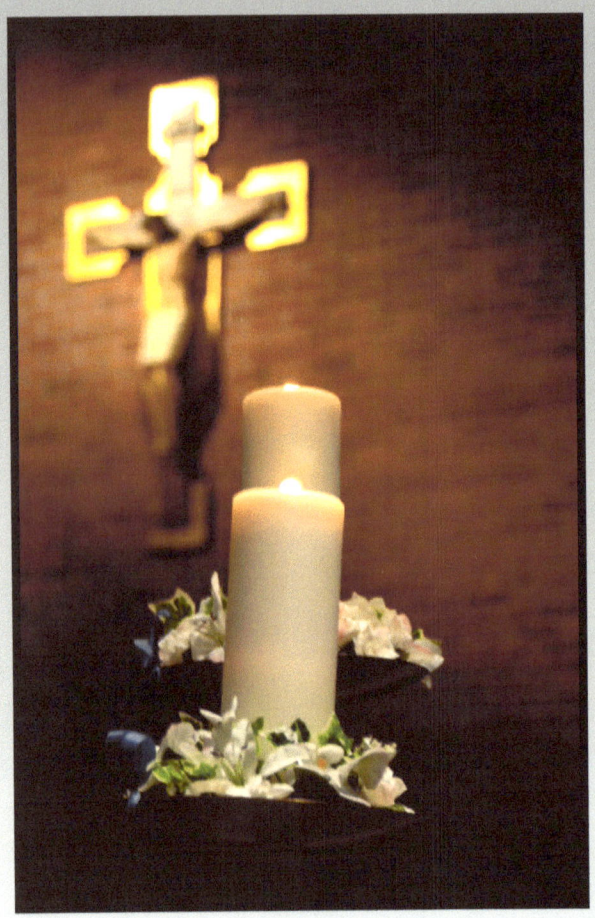

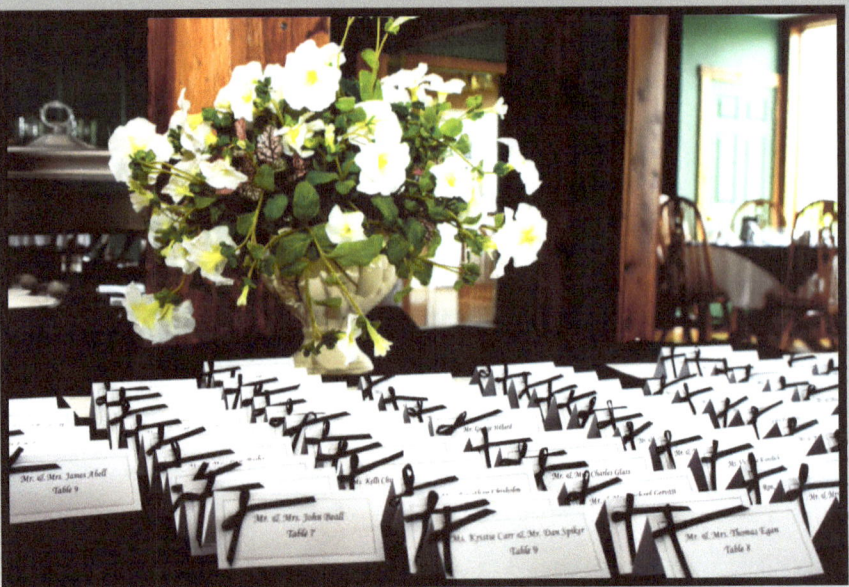

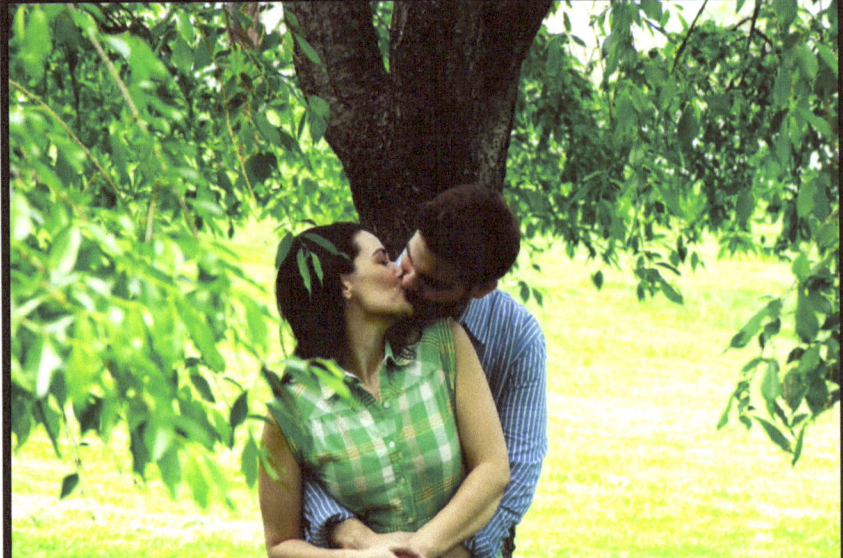

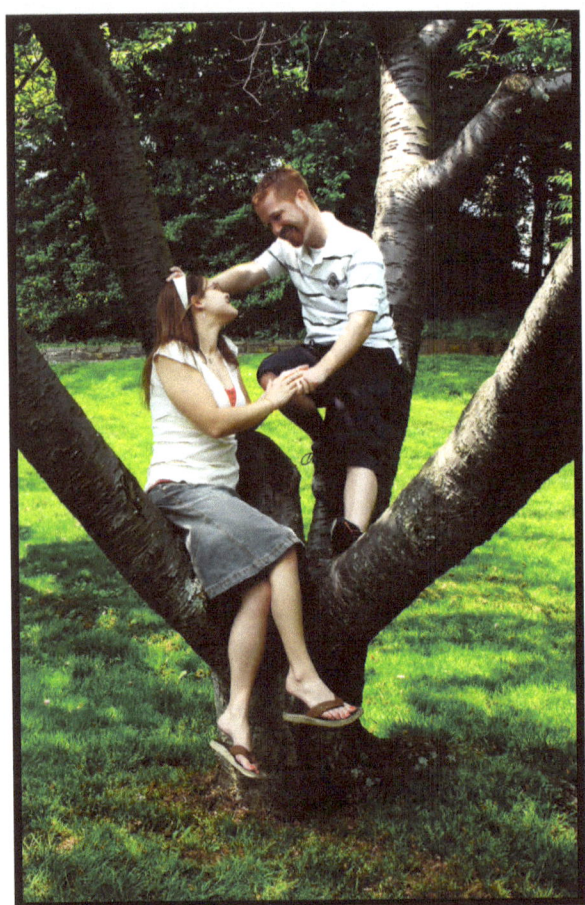

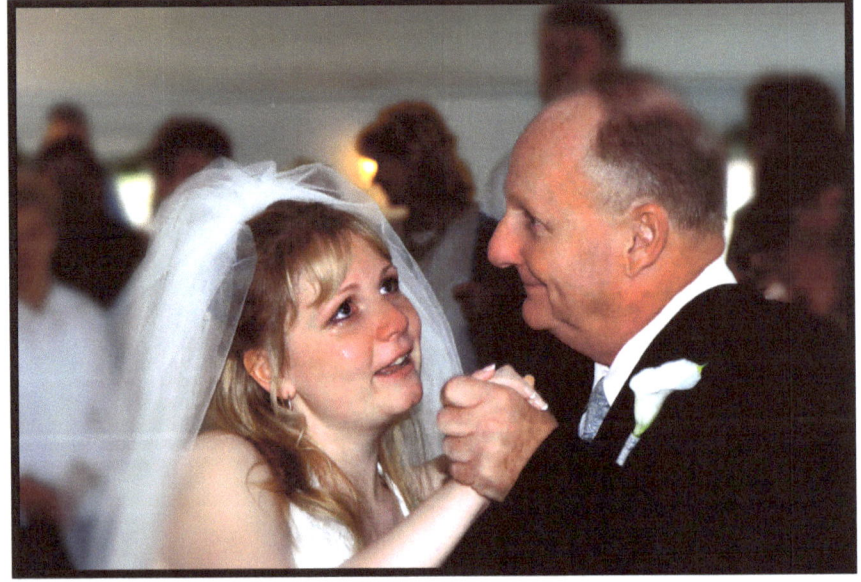

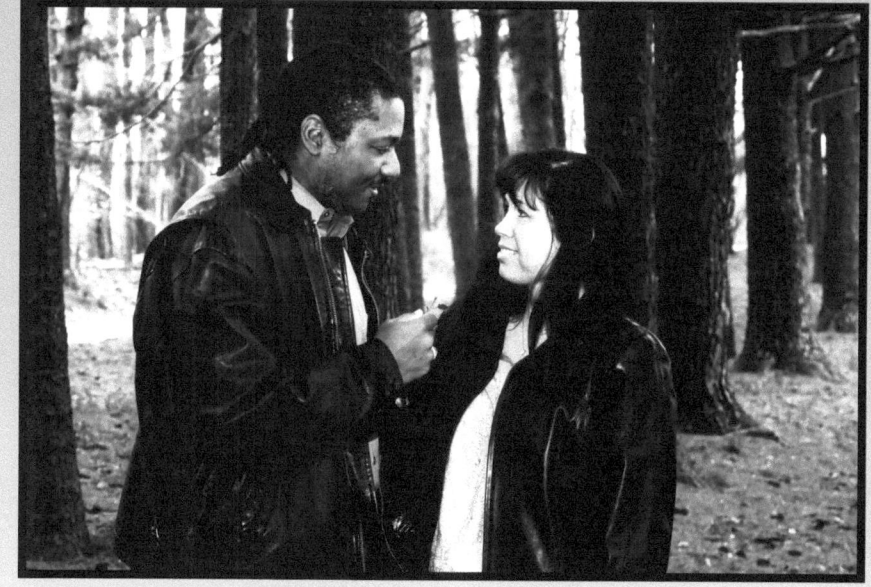

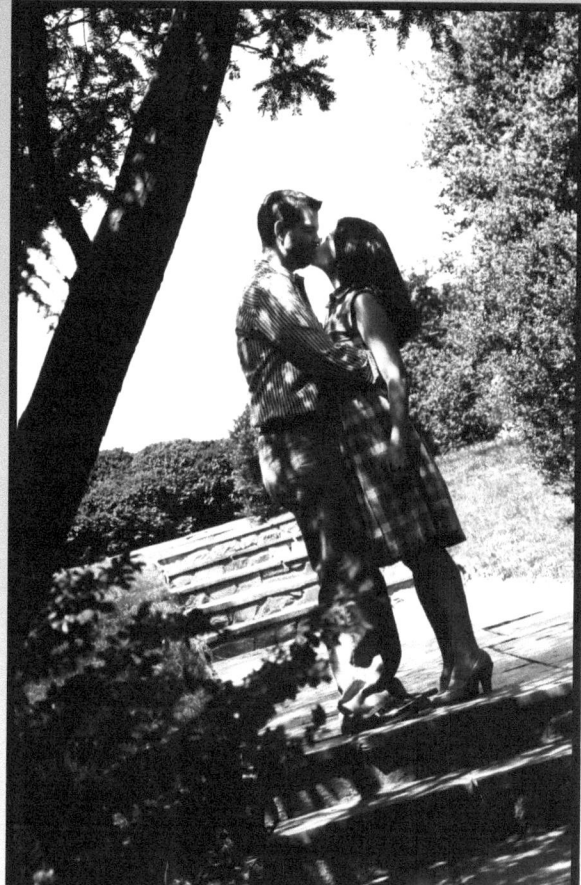

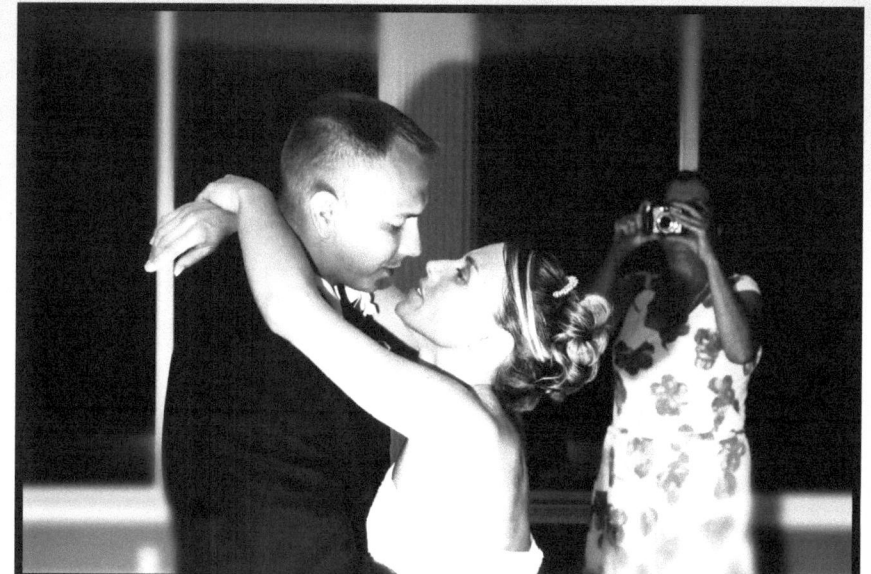

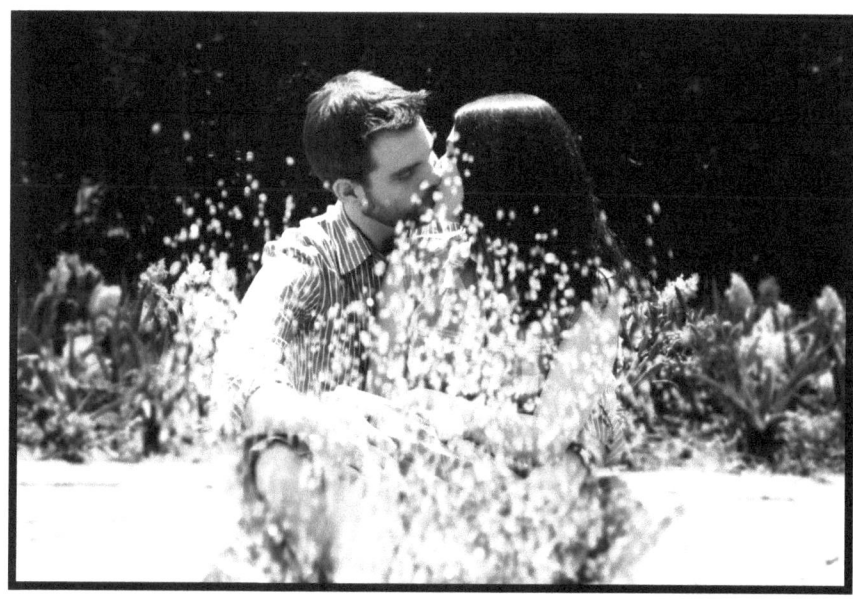

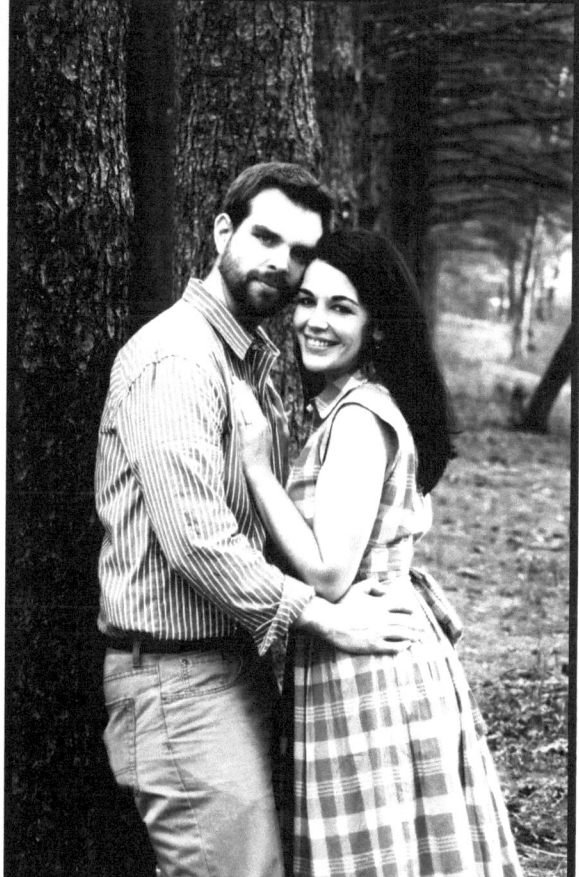

With everything that is going on, you may miss many of the fine details of your wedding day, such as the beautiful decorations, your bridal party having a moment, etc. We have learned to have eyes in the back of our heads to ensure nothing is missed throughout the day. We love the wow factor....when our clients tell us that they didn't know that happened or they didn't know we took that!

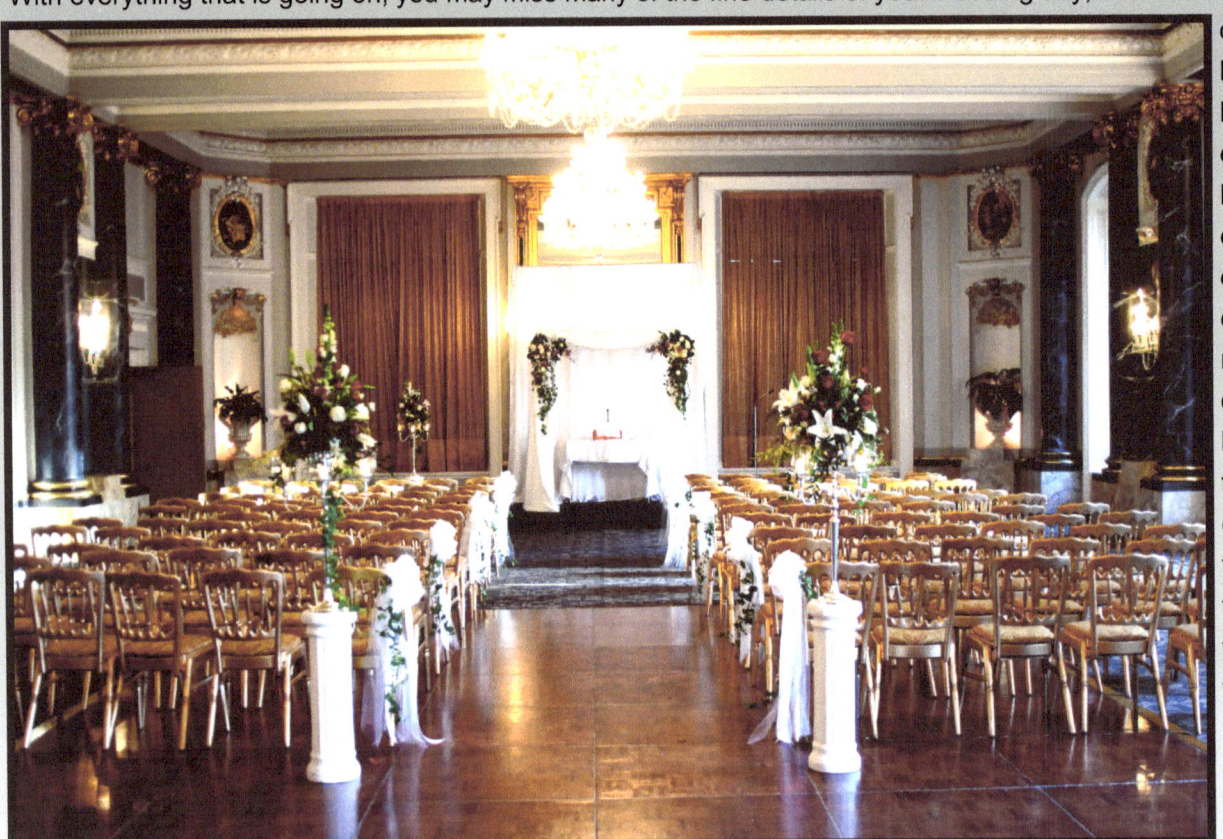

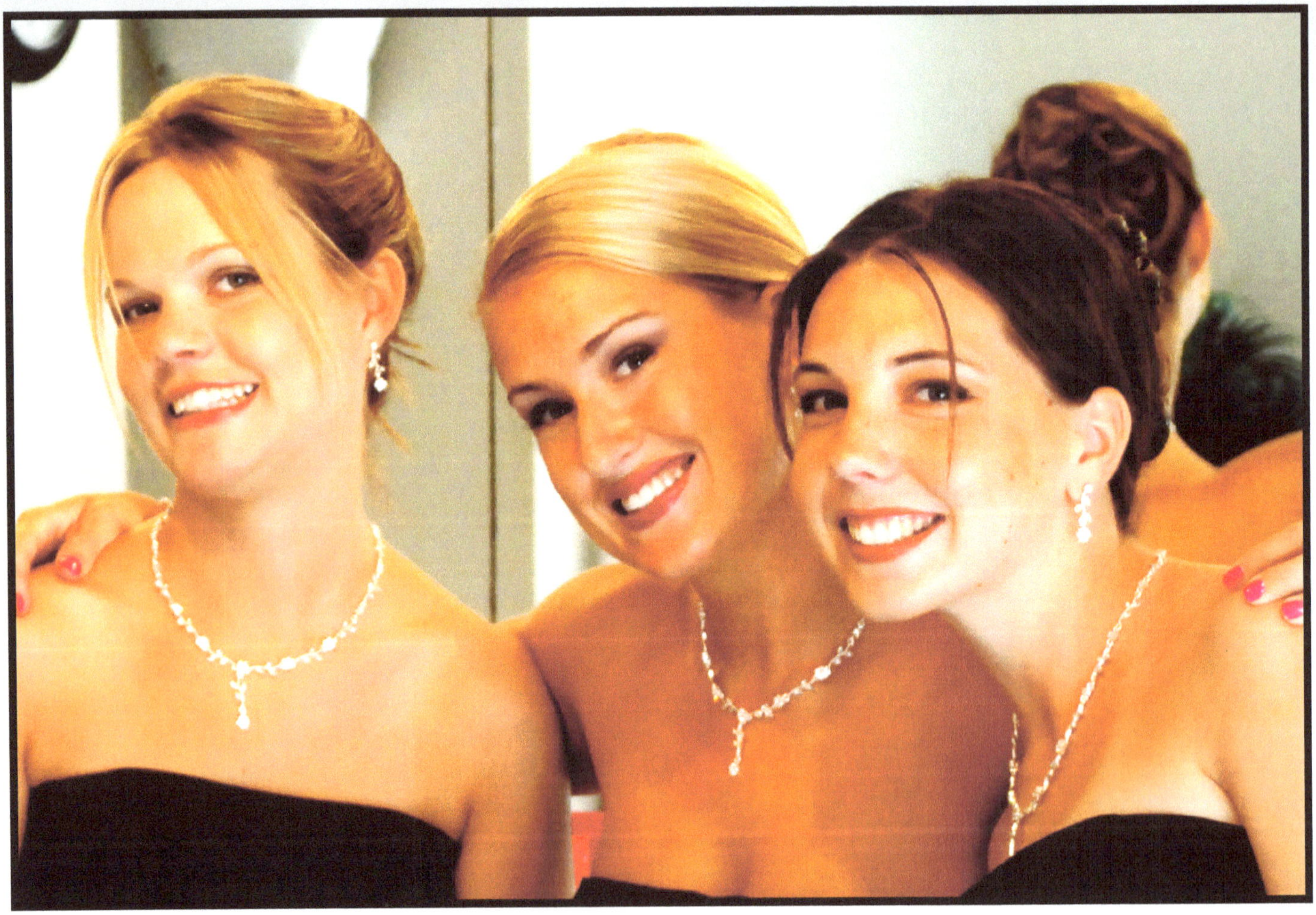

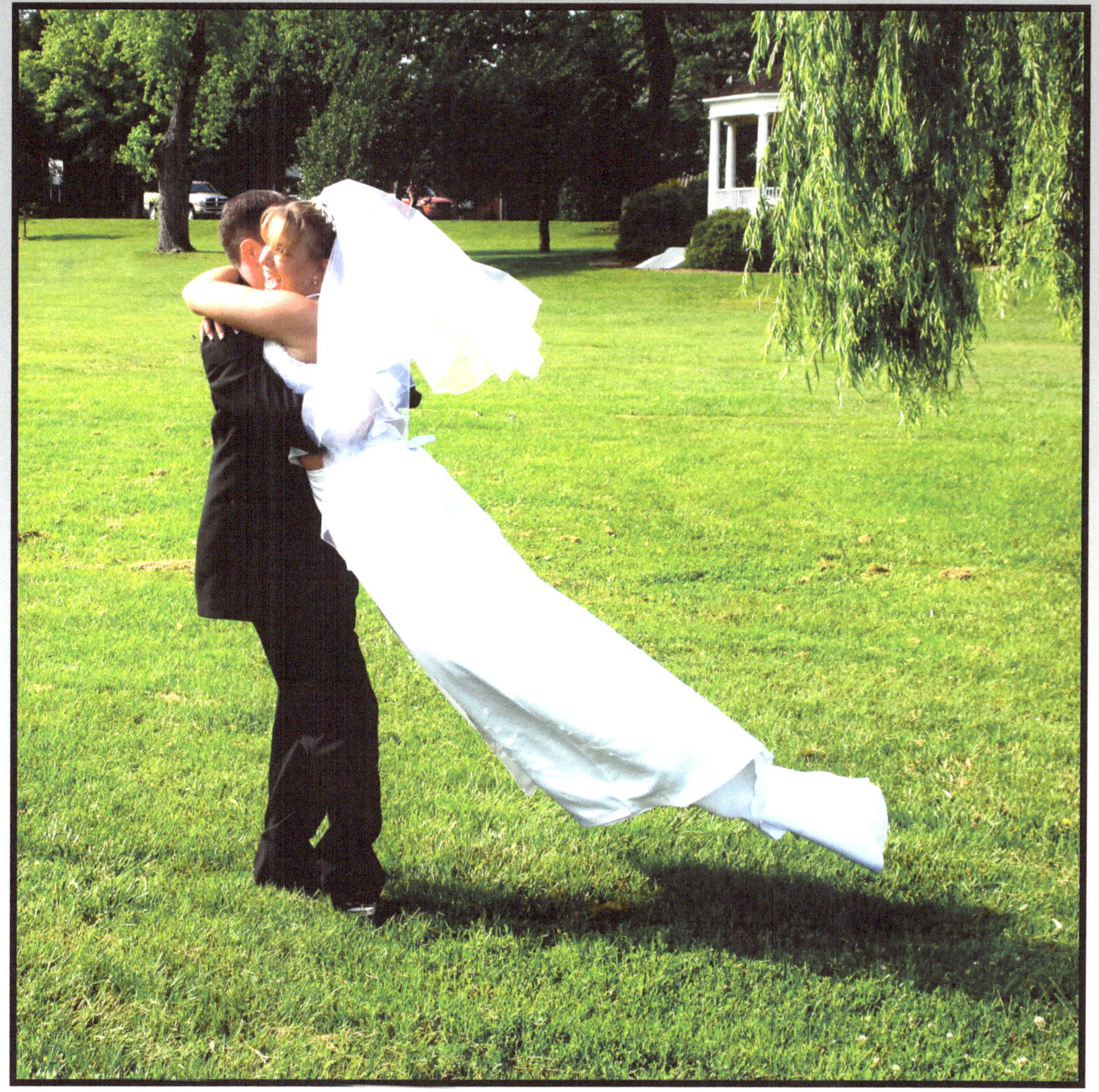

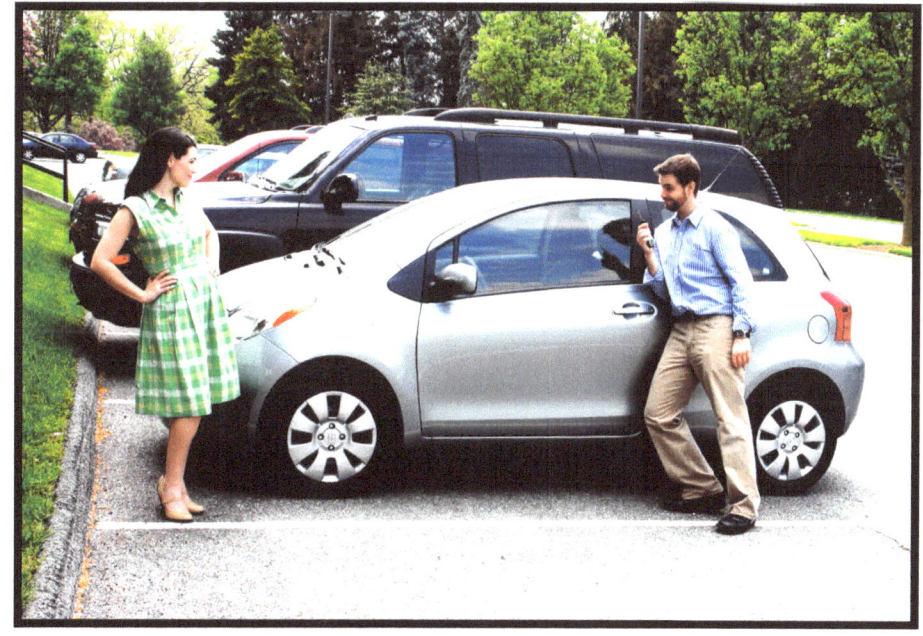

Don't pass up opportunities to express what makes you unique.

Photos such as these will often turn out to be your most treasured memories of the day!

So just be sure to relax and be who are! We will capture it all!

Enjoy your day and have fun with it!

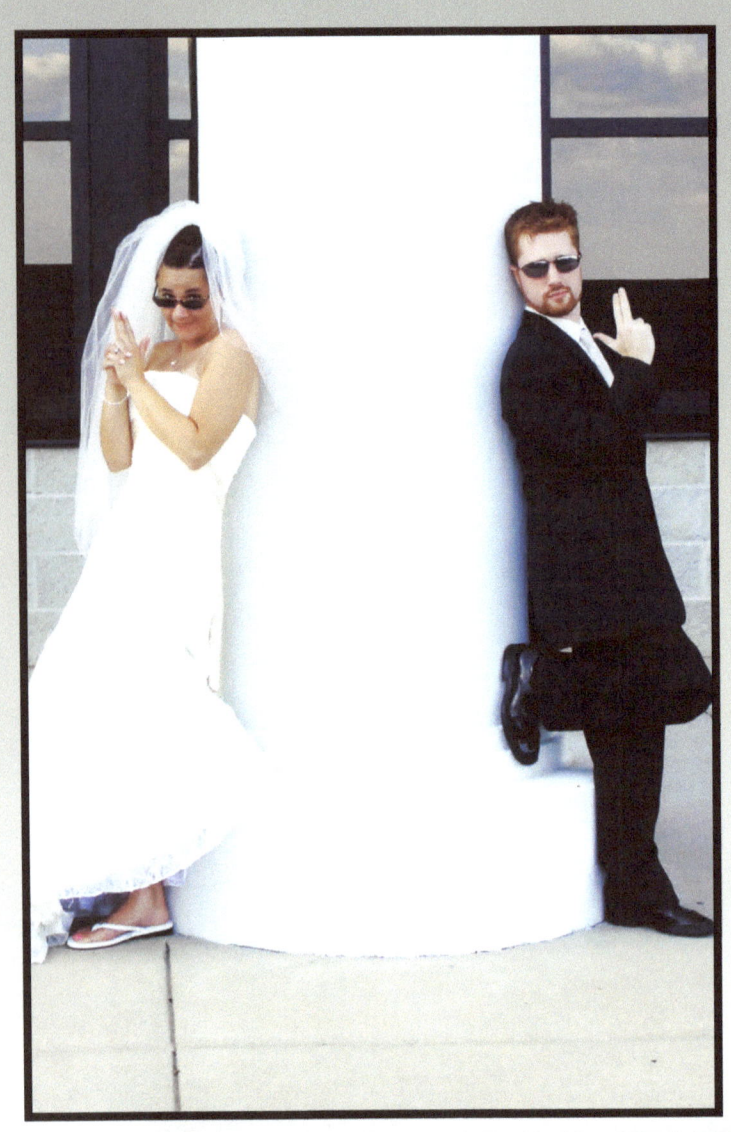

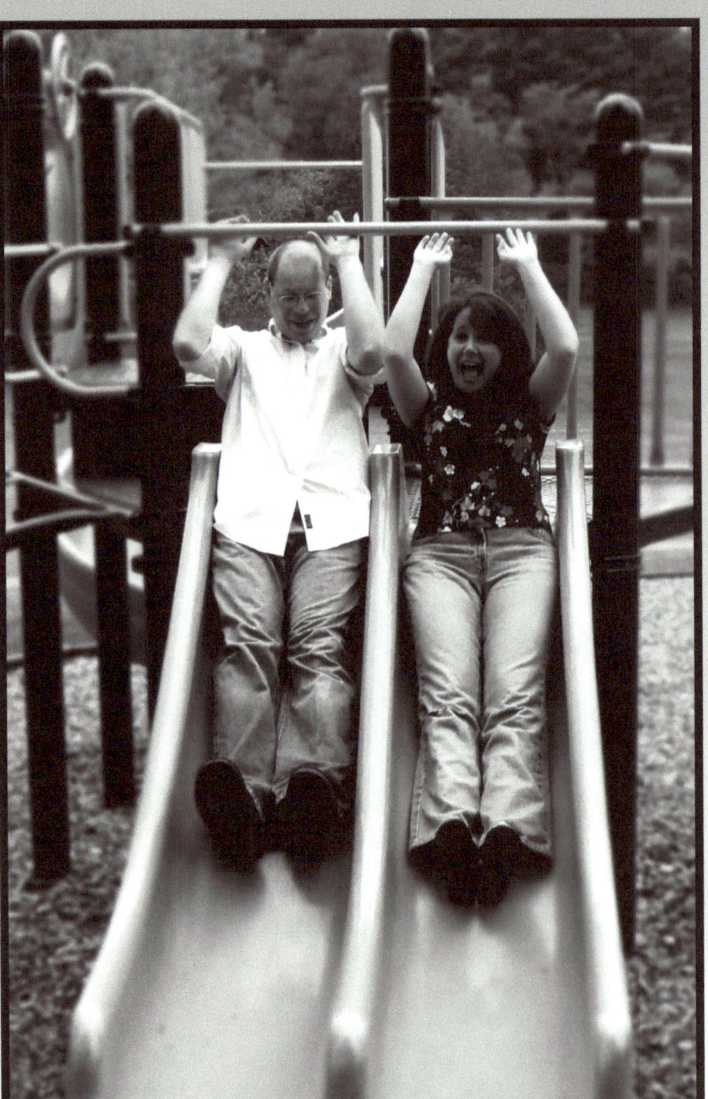

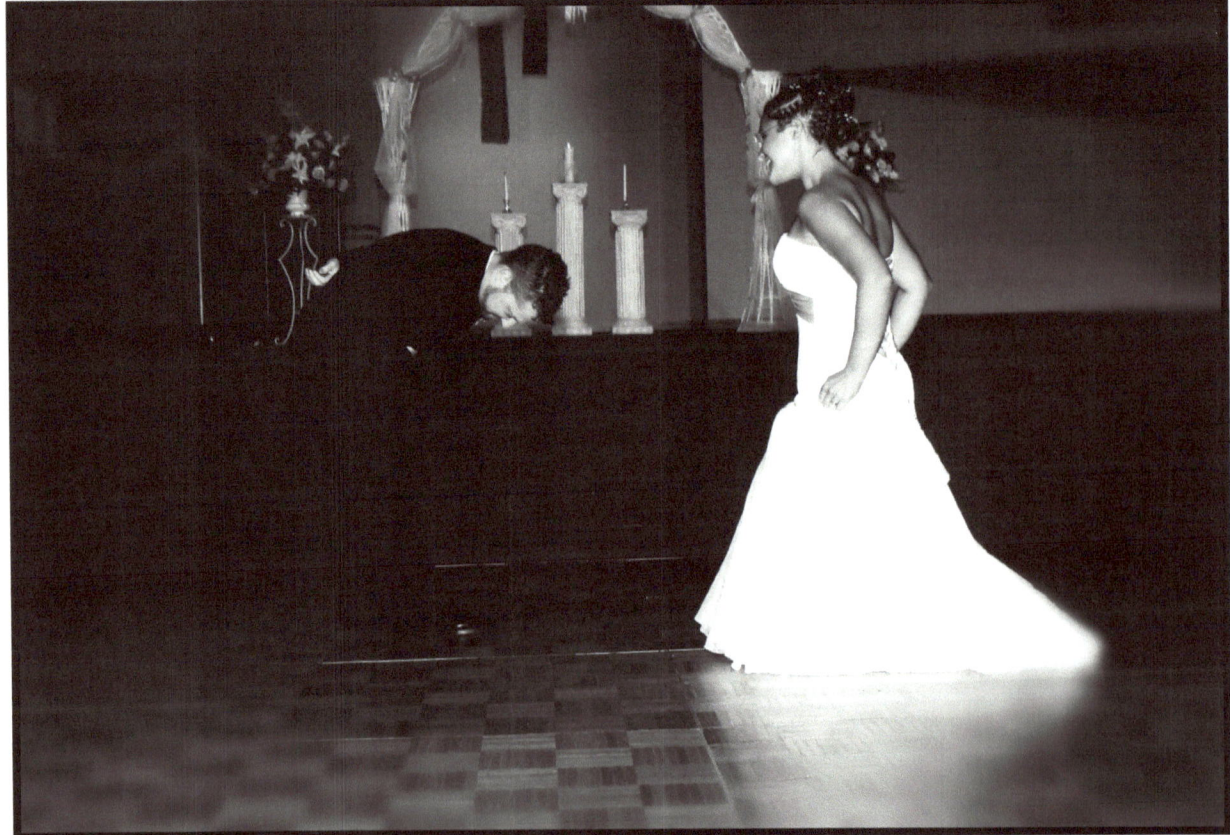

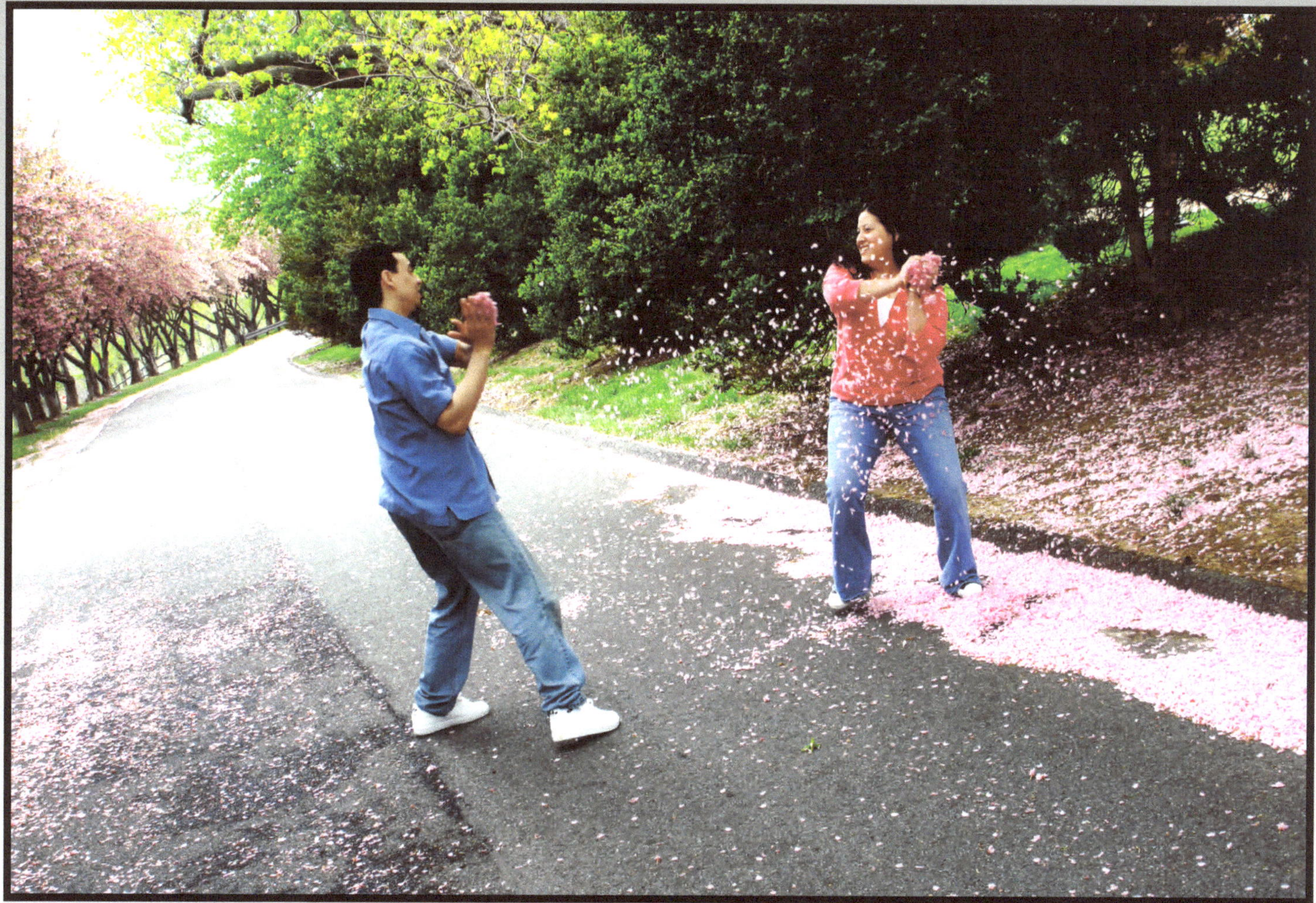

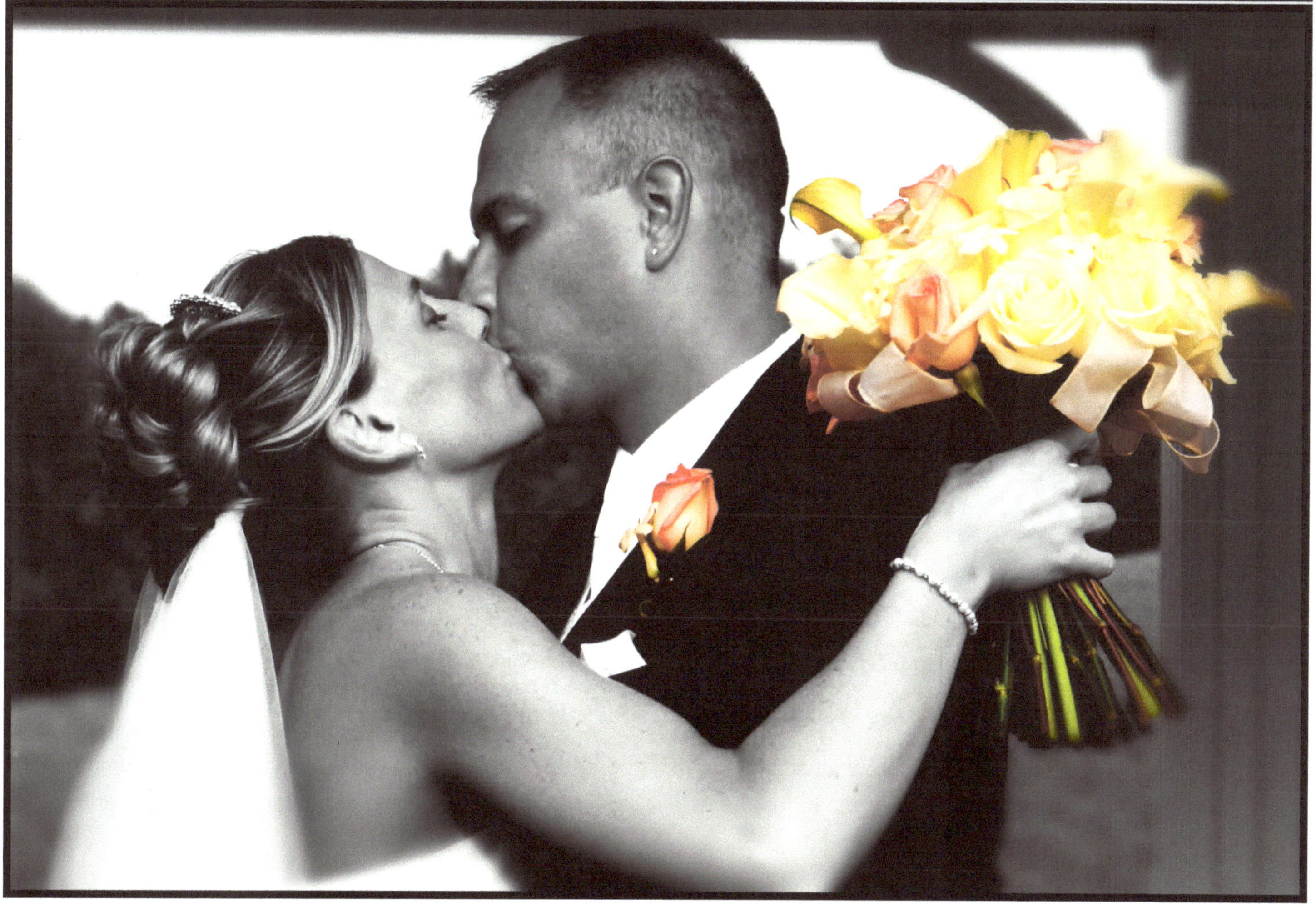

Be the best that you can

There are some tricks you should know that can make you, your wedding party, and your family look better in photographs! For the most part, these secrets about how to pose yourself are optical illusions, usually caused by the fact that the camera uses a single lens as opposed to your two eyes.....the tips are easy and might be like a painless diet...and we all know about diets! If we can tell you that you can look ten pounds thinner simply by standing a certain way, we are certain that you would jump at the chance. By knowing these tips and practicing prior to your wedding day, you can look your absolute best in your photographs.....

Moms know best

Almost every mom said to her daughter to point a toe when posing for a photo. By pointing your toe, you are shifting your weight to your back foot, which in turn causes your hips to shift. This hip shifting will emphasize your curves. The goal is to make you look sexy, but with an innocent appearance. Always try to avoid placing your feet together while flat on the ground.

Stand up straight with good posture

This may seem obvious, but something as ordinary as standing straight can do wonders for your image. Don't slouch, you look more confident and sure of yourself when you stand with good posture.

Relax your shoulders

Hunching your shoulders makes your neck look shorter. When you relax your shoulders, you will look more natural and less tense on your most special day.

Position your shoulders at a 45 degree angle to the camera

If you turn your body slightly to the right or left, you can shave off 10 pounds or so on camera....

If you wear glasses

1. Photo-gray lenses are a big no-no!!! They darken when outdoors ......even when you are inside, they appear very dark in photographs.

2. There are non-glare lenses that you can put in your existing frames for relatively little cost. While not 100% effective, they help reduce reflections.

3. If possible, the lenses should tilt slightly downwards so the flash will be reflected towards the ground and not back at the camera. This trick can also be accomplished by lowering your chin slightly.

   - When wearing glasses, a simple and slight nod downward will help cut glare.

   - If you are on the edge of deciding on getting contacts, it would be a great time to make the jump before your big day! Take it from someone who recently made the transition to contacts..."getting contacts is the best decision I have made." - Craig

Relax your forehead

Don't try to open your eyes too wide. This can create unwanted furrows in your forehead. It is better to keep your eyes and forehead relaxed in order to look more natural.

Try not to squint

While taking outdoor photographs, the sun may be out and will cause you to squint. Try to keep your eyes slightly closed when lining up and open your eyes when the photographer counts down for the photograph.

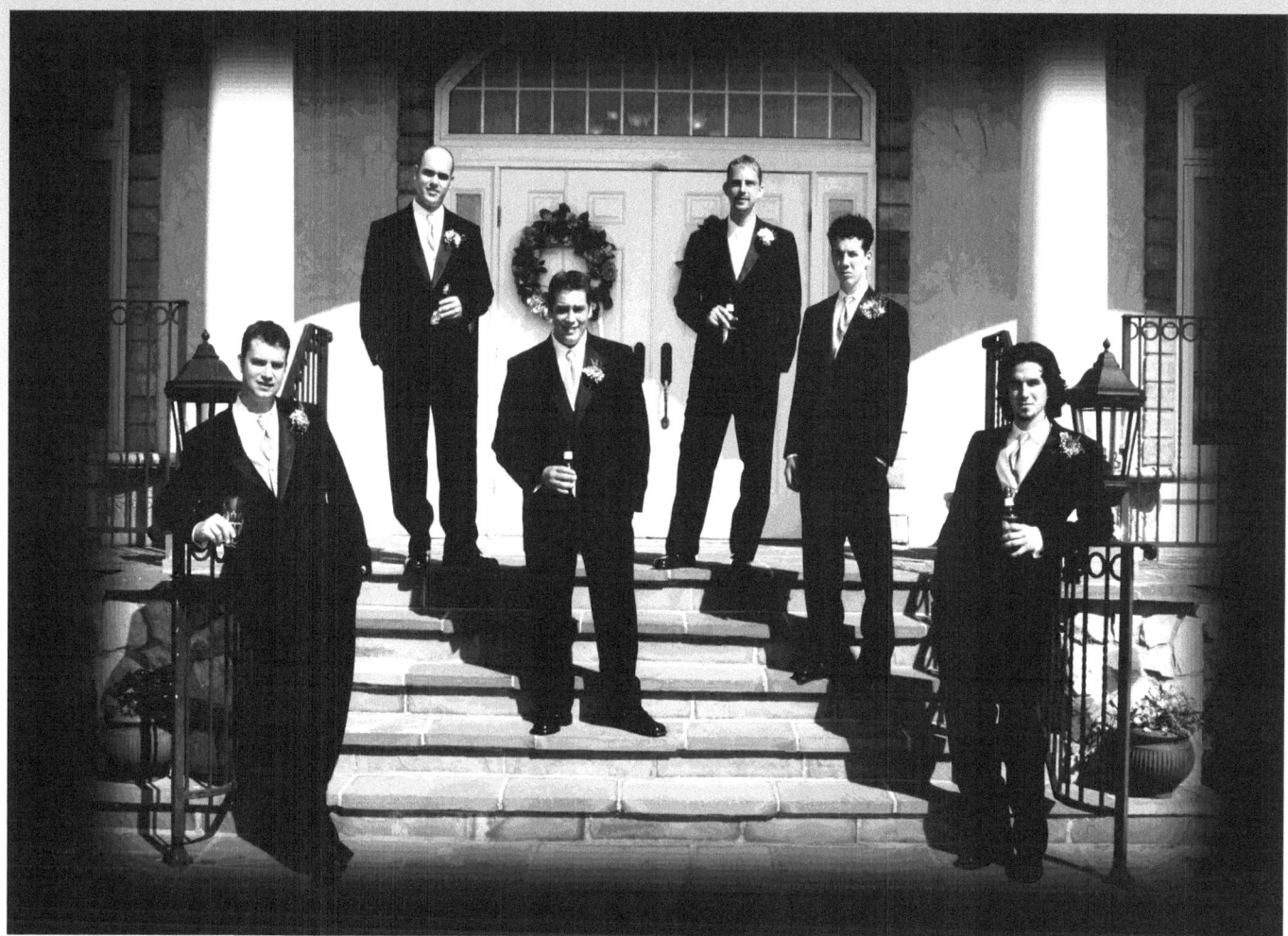

Be yourself!

When posing for a photograph, act natural and show your true emotions!

Important words

All the suggestions and tricks about posing should be used sparingly. In almost every case, overdoing a good thing can result in disaster. Your application of these ideas should be measured in fractions of an inch. To help test your posing, stand in front of a mirror and look at yourself. Now lower your chin 1/4 of an inch. Then try it again but this time lower your chin a full inch. In the first case, you'll hardly notice the difference in the mirror, but in your photos your eyes will look larger. The second instance will result in photos that show a double chin.

No one trick is going to magically transform you from full-figured to a super-model. However, by using all of them….each will help improve your posing techniques a bit and will enhance your photographs.

Hide those double-chins

Don't pull your head towards your neck while standing straight. This will accentuate the lines of a double chin. Rather, the key is to lean forward at the waist while slightly tilting your head backwards.

Look flattering

It is usually less flattering to lift your head back because your chin becomes more prominent than your eyes. Instead, lower your chin to tilt your forehead ever so slightly closer to the camera. This emphasizes the attractiveness of your eyes. It is also a good idea to lick your lips before a photograph. This will add a shiny look!

Even the groom should get a manicure

Two people with well-manicured hands create photo opportunities beyond the typical "ring shot." However, if you do not have time to get one or forget… no worries, we can give you a manicure in Photoshop ;0)

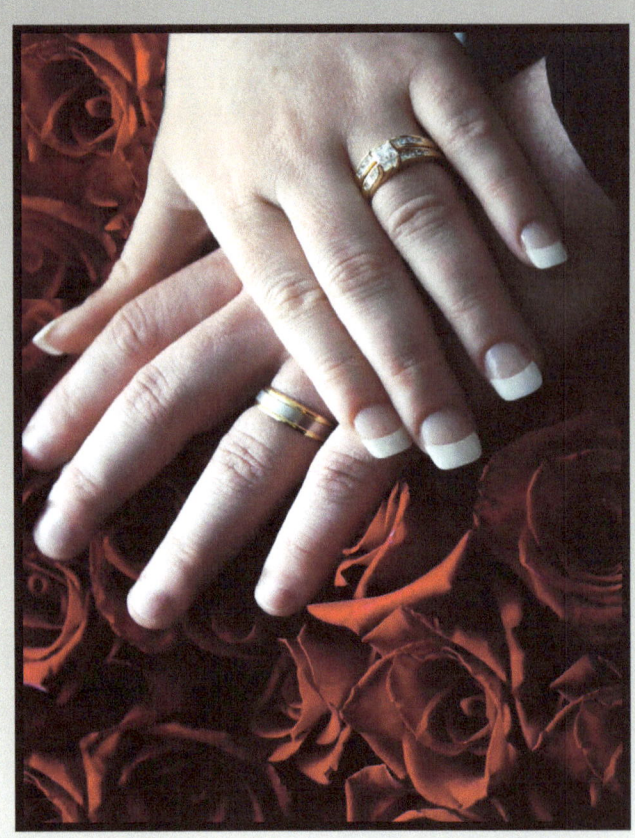

Makeup

Your wedding day is not the day to experiment with makeup or a new hairstyle. Your day and pictures that will be with you for at least the next fifty years + is too important to take a gamble with. We suggest that you stick with a style that you already know works for you, or experiment with styles a few months prior to the big day! When you are looking at your makeup, remember, things in the mirror always look different in person than in a photograph. It is a good idea to ask your photographer to take some test shots of your makeup ideas and hair.

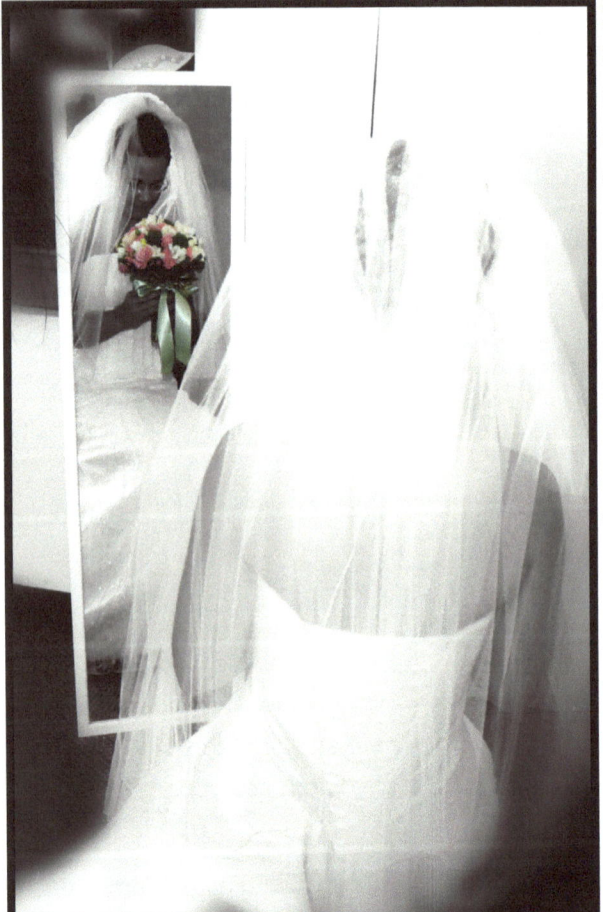

Holding the bouquet

Please don't hide yourself or your dress behind your flowers. Always try to hold the bouquet low with your wrists on your hip.

A note for romantics

Many years back when Kathy and I were dating, she gave me a single rose. I dried the rose and preserved it in cellophane wrap. To this day, I still have it and look at it from time to time. If you plan to throw your bouquet at the reception, try getting an artificial duplicate and use that one so you can preserve the one you used!

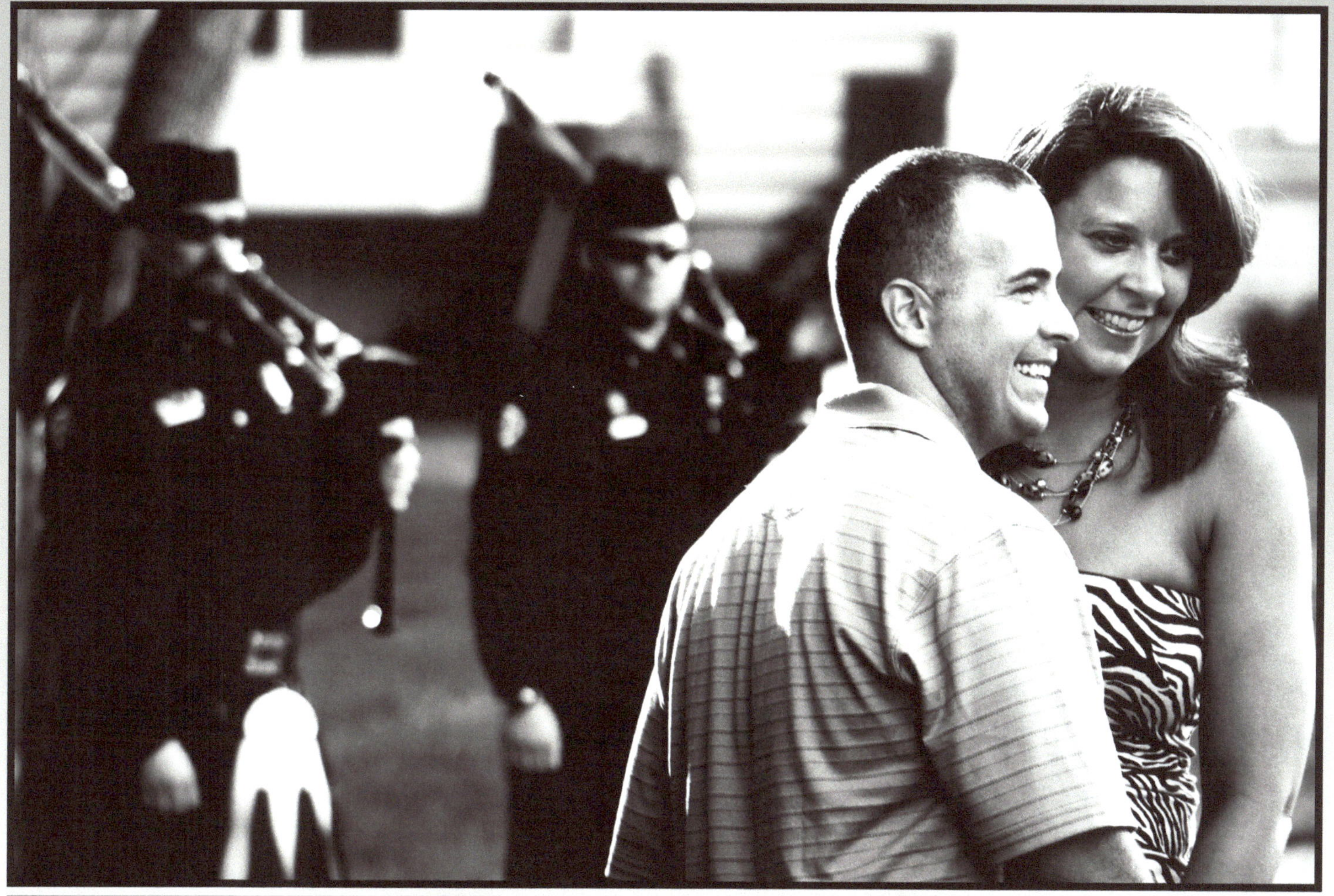

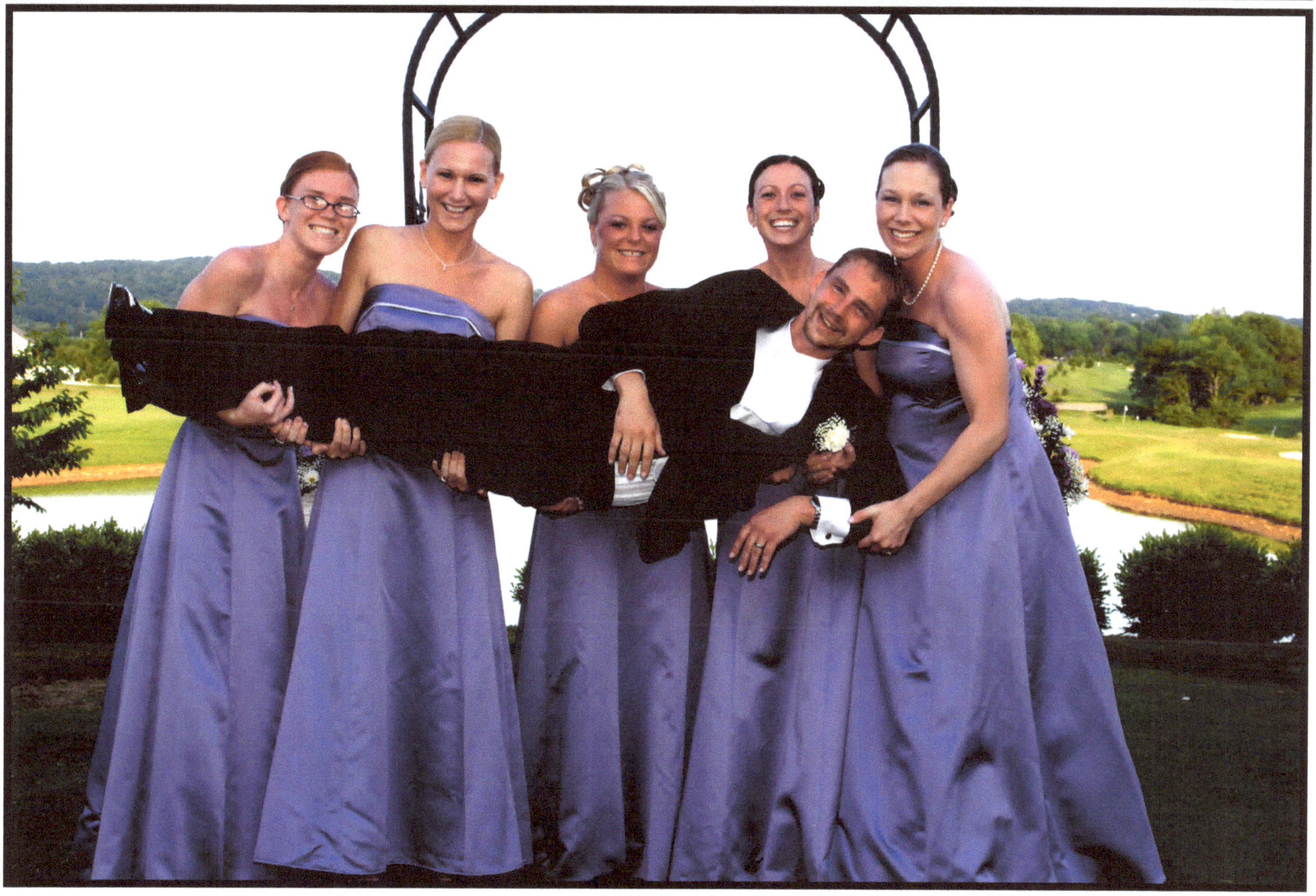

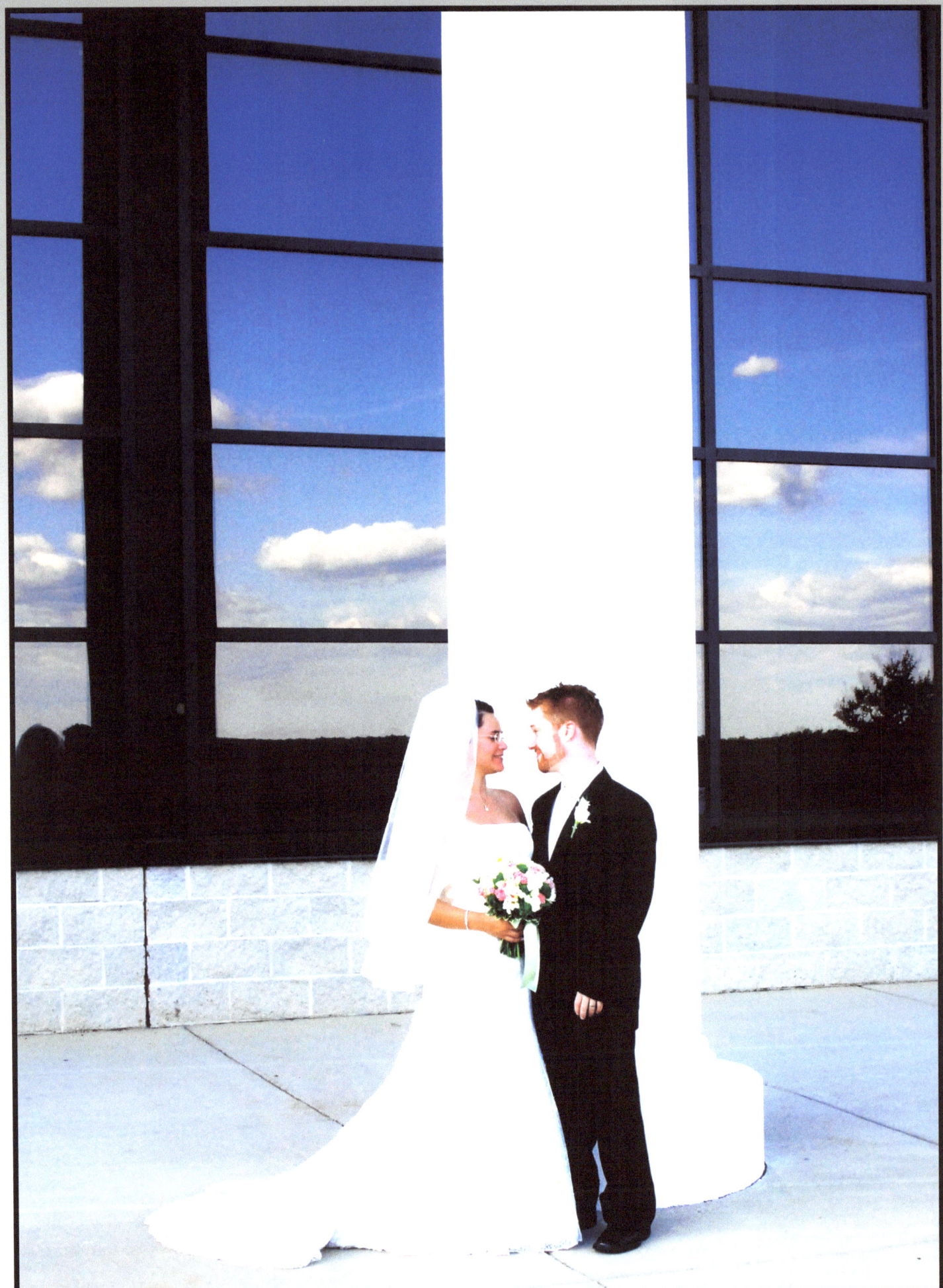

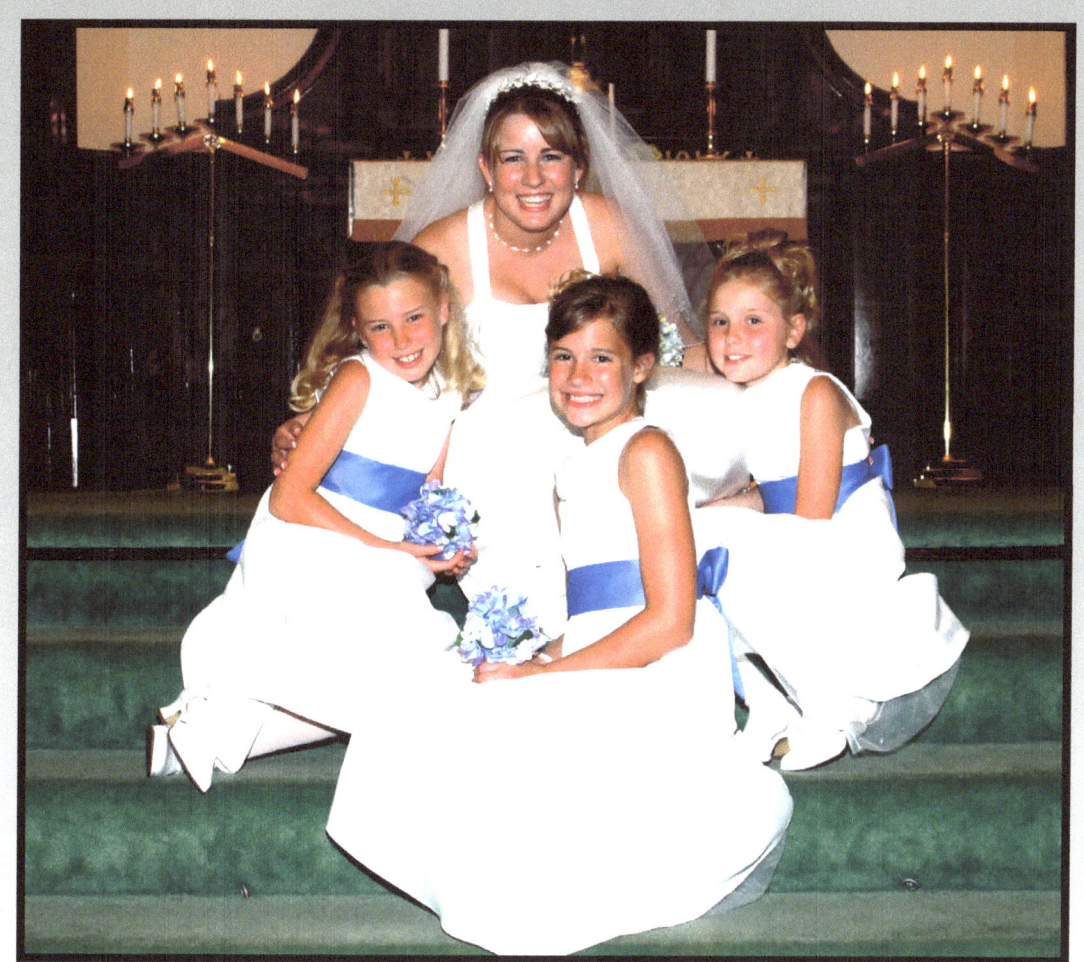

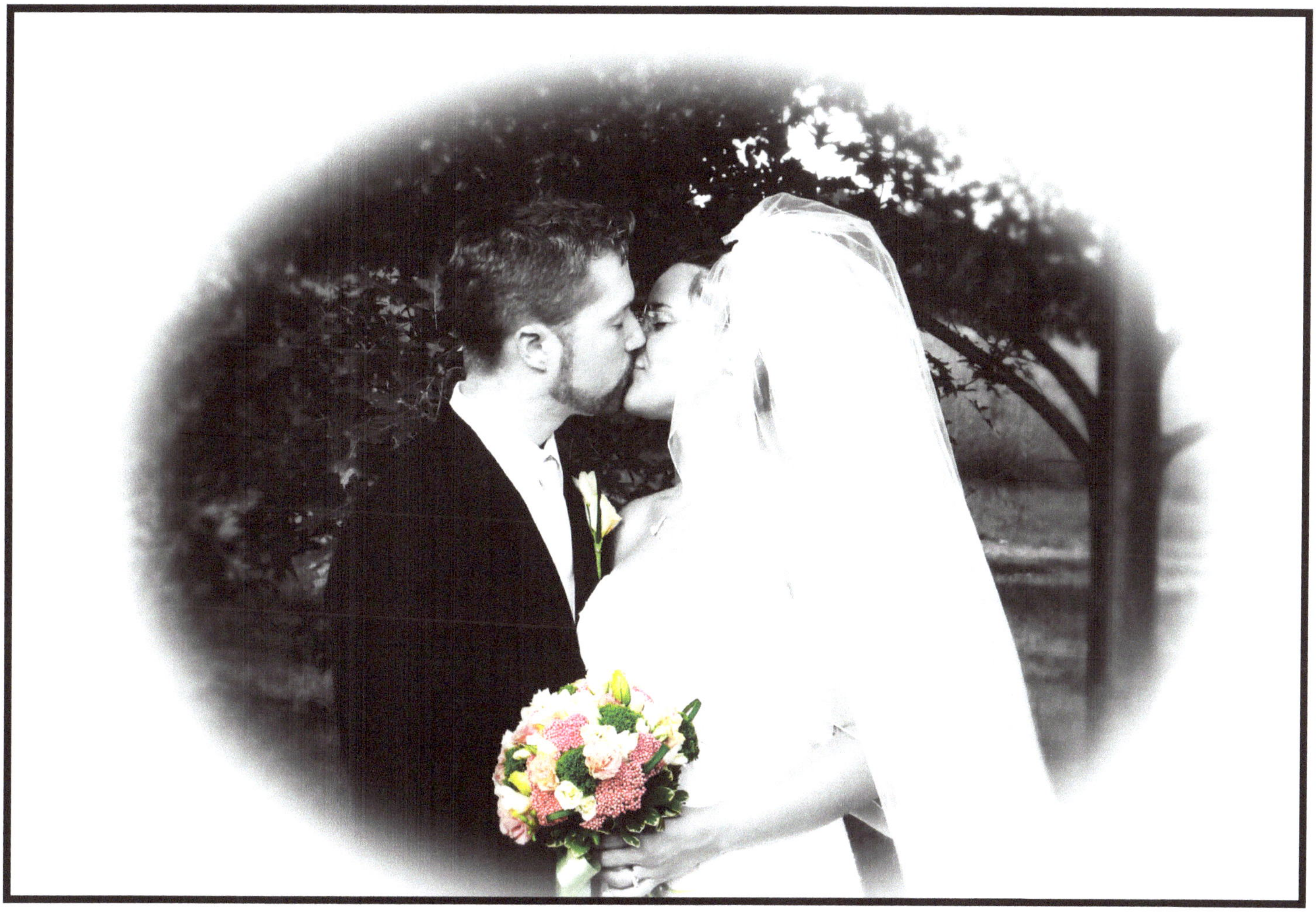

It's going to be a L-O-N-G day

A typical wedding day will run a total of 8 or more hours start to finish for the bride, groom , bridal party and photographer and 4-6 hours for guests. It is common for a dinner reception to begin four or more hours after the start of the ceremony so hide snacks incase you have an appetite, eat something a few hours before getting ready and prepare yourself in advance for a long and tiresome day.

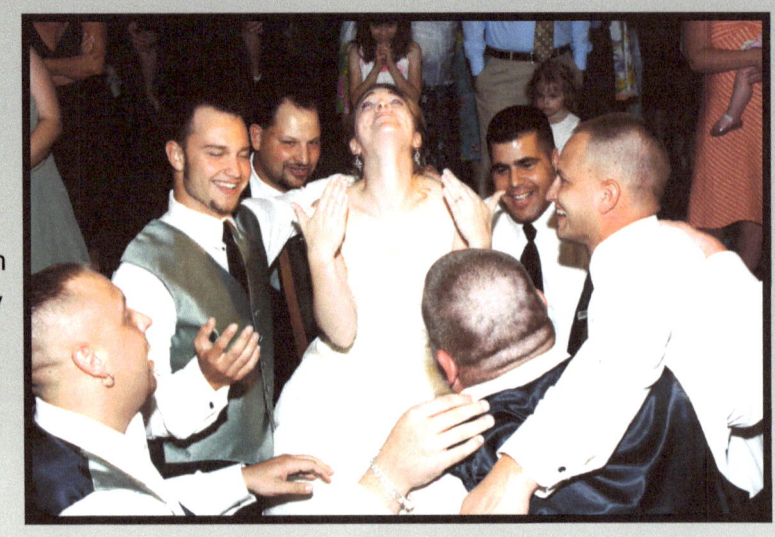

Pinning on a boutonnière

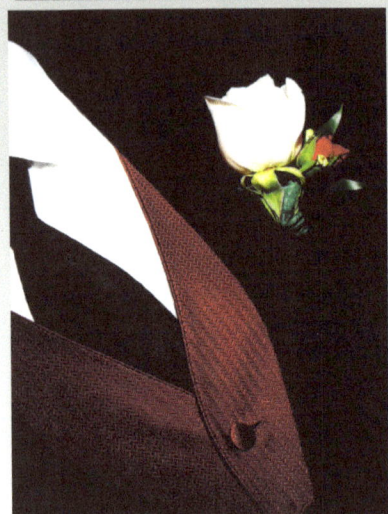

Brides– since you are not with the guys when they pin on the boutonnières....we thought you would like to know what is going on in the other room: the guys open the box, look at the flowers and pins and become completely helpless.... Hopefully, the groom's mom or someone with past experience is nearby and will lend a helping hand. Otherwise, the guys will stick the pins through the flowers and then jab them into their chests, drawing blood or causing some sort of pain to one another. I can't tell you how many times we had to step in and save the guys from getting all bloody and or destroying their boutonnieres! Brides.....here is a little tidbit that can help a bit. It's really simple. Have your fiancé get a jacket and practice pinning a boutonnière on the lapel with the jacket off. Then on the wedding day, your fiancé will know how to do this and can showoff to his friends! Boutonnières always go on the left lapel of the jacket. With a little practice, they are relatively simple to pin on!

Please keep in mind…...

Remember that photographers are not mind readers. The only way to insure that you get photos of important traditions

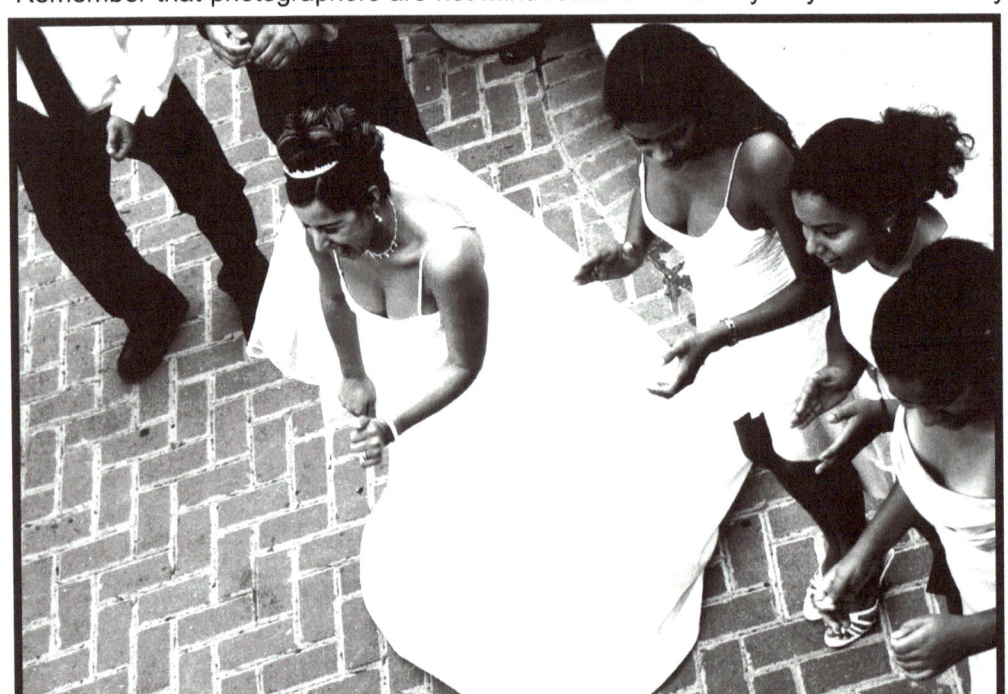

or special family members and friends is to inform us ahead of time about special activities that you want photographed. Most activities are easy for us to catch, but special customs such as your family and friend forming an arch for you to run through on the dance floor can happen and end in matter of seconds. We have strong intuitions and keen eyes for detail and will capture almost everything, but a little warning would be nice!

Why digital?

We like to refer to digital photography as "digitally mastered photographs." As skilled Photoshop craftsmen, we can alter, darken, lighten, add or take away contrast, enhance, and almost do any changes you may want to your photographs. Some people are skeptical about digitally enhanced photography. Just look at it this way, the computer is a digital darkroom and it takes just as much skill as it would in the dark with film, and the finished product looks a lot better. One second after taking an image, our camera will display the image on a 2.5 inch LCD screen located on the back of the camera. We can instantly double check lighting, composition and posing! This is one of the biggest advantages to digital we have experienced yet! Keep in mind that most people are using standard digital cameras that are very limited in the functions that are offered and priced somewhere around the $300 - $1000.00 range. Not all digital cameras are alike. We use several digital, professional SLR cameras that have more functions then a professional film camera and are priced from $6,000 +, not including any accessories and lenses.

❑ The ability to see the image right away. This is our favorite reason for using digital. It gives us a level of comfort because we can see if the lighting, expression, exposure, etc. are correct right away rather than wait to see the film back from the lab in a few days.

❑ The ability to change the ISO (or the equivalent of film speed) quickly. This allows us to go in and out of an array of lighting situations without having to suddenly change film to match the light levels from place to place at a wedding.

❑ A virtually unlimited number of photographs can be captured at an event. This in its self frees us from thinking "we can only shoot 10, 12 or whatever number of rolls of film that is in the client's budget".

❑ The ability to make black and white and sepia toned photographs from the digital images. When we shoot digital, every photograph can become a black and white and/or sepia image. Parents may want an image in color; the couple may want to have it in black and white.

❑ Freedom to experiment. We will often shoot images that we would not even try with film because with digital, we will be able to erase it if it doesn't work and modify it because we'll be seeing the results immediately.

❑ Most of all, the ability to have unlimited editing. Imagine having an ugly light switch behind a beautiful wedding cake in every photograph (see images below)! With today's technology, the sky is the limit in what can be done with a photograph. This is where Kathy's forte comes in...she has an impeccable eye for detail, the skill and patience to ensure that every photograph is edited perfectly and a work of art! Stay tuned for our upcoming Photoshop workbooks and online photography training courses....

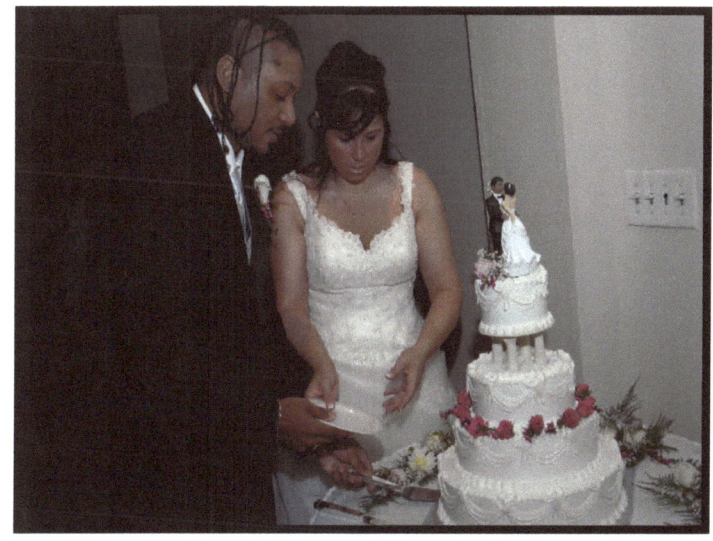 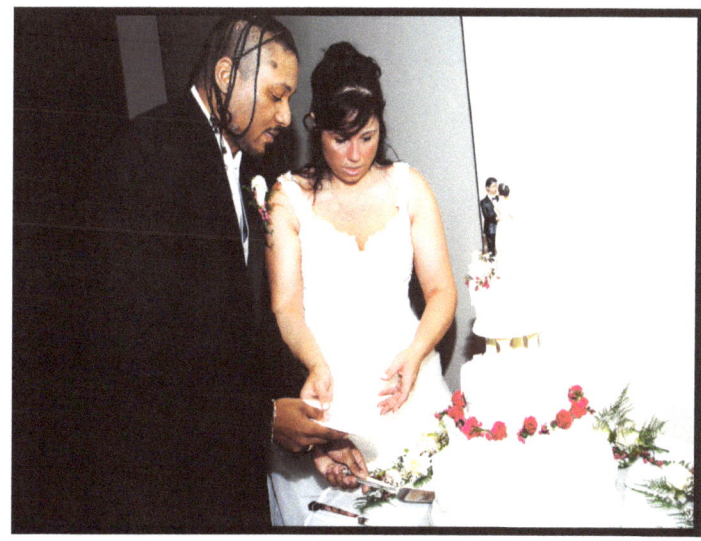

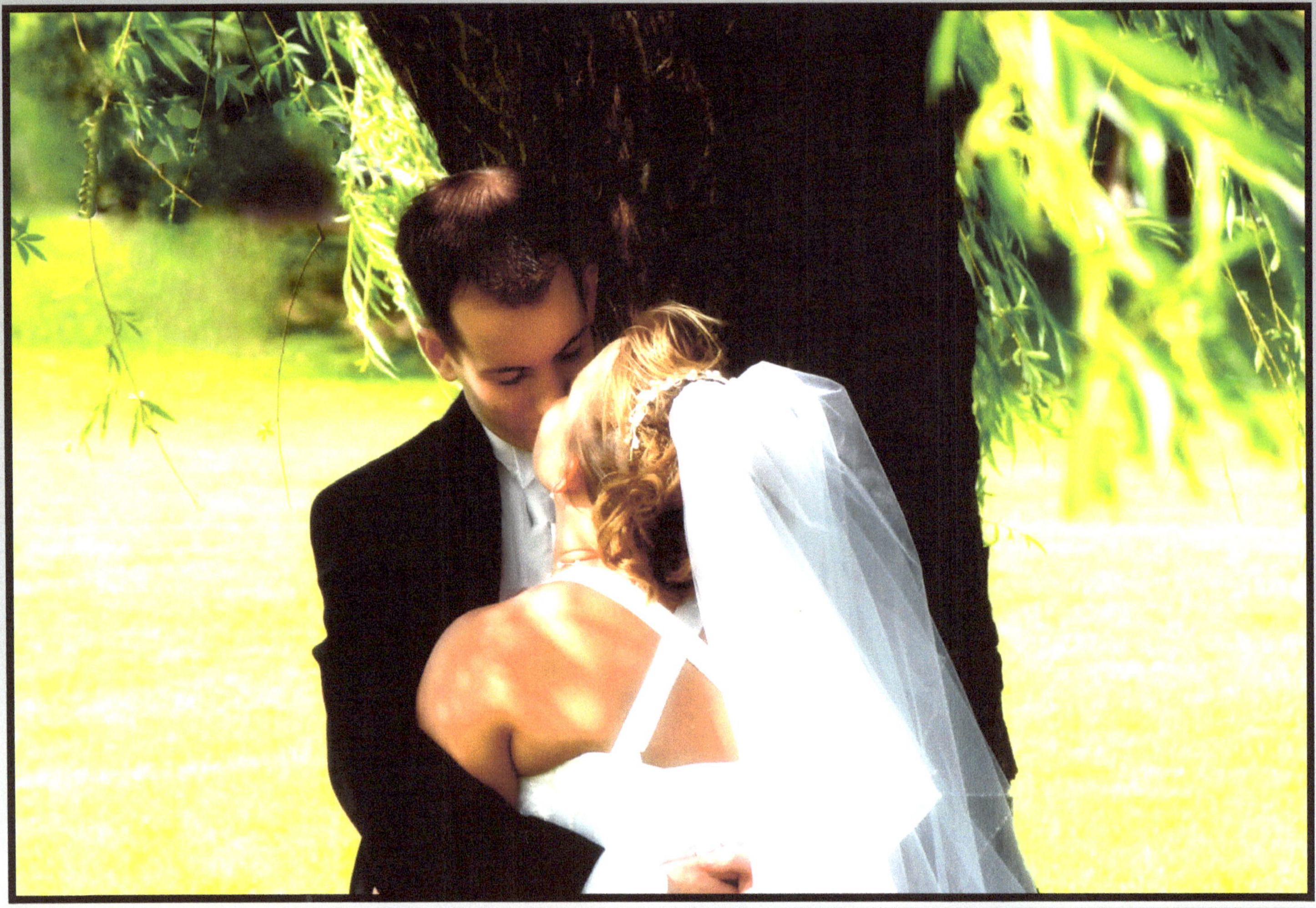

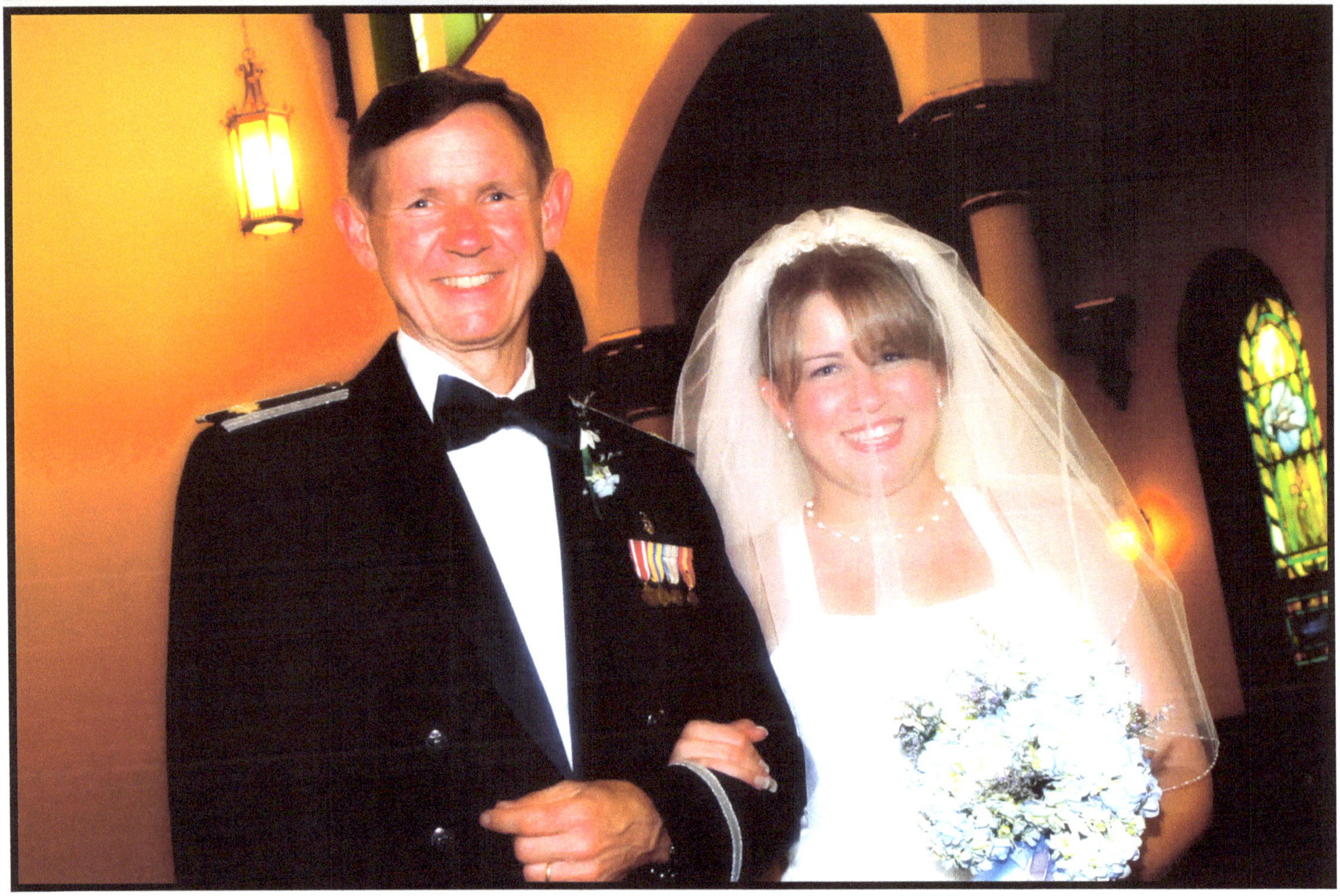

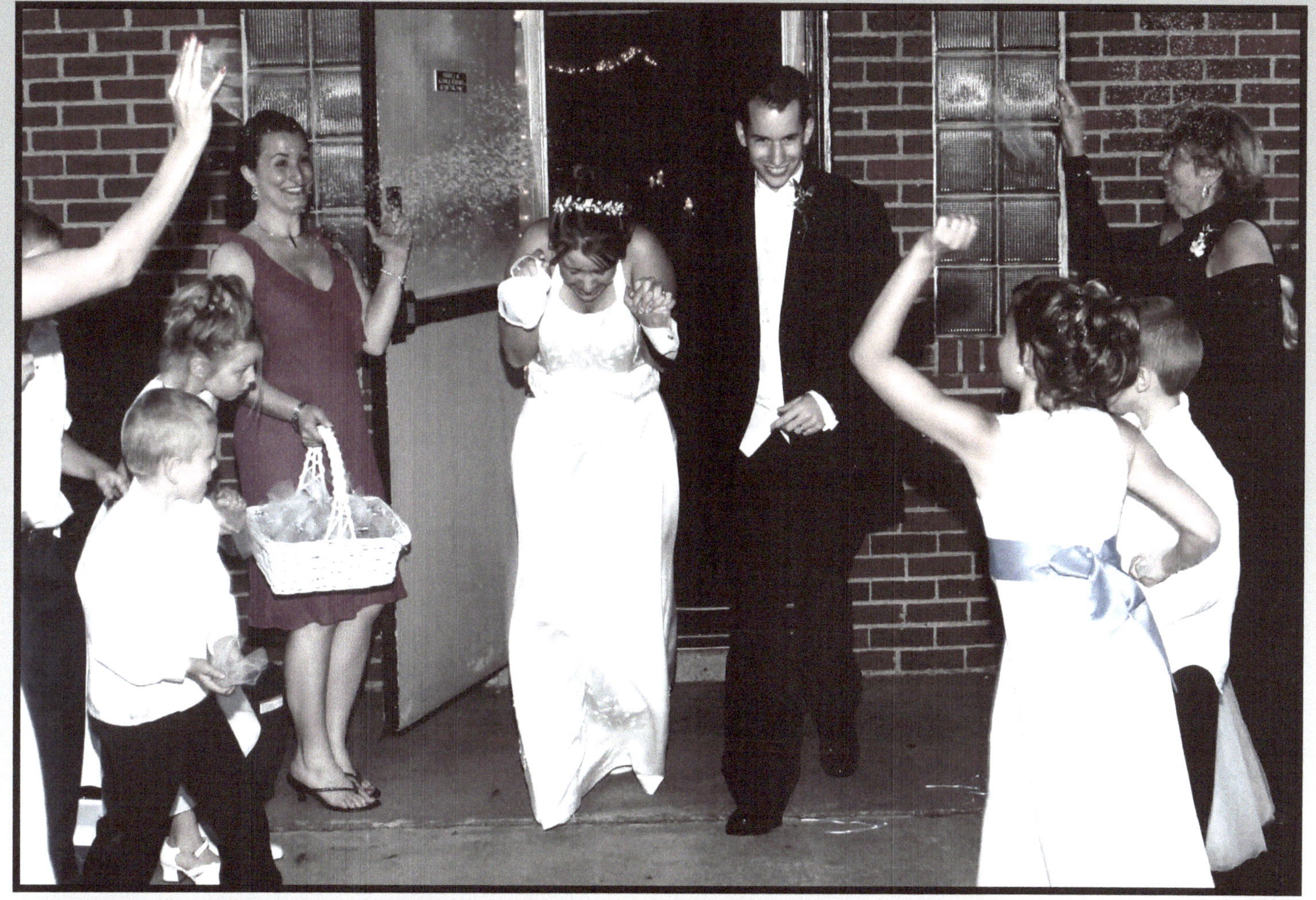

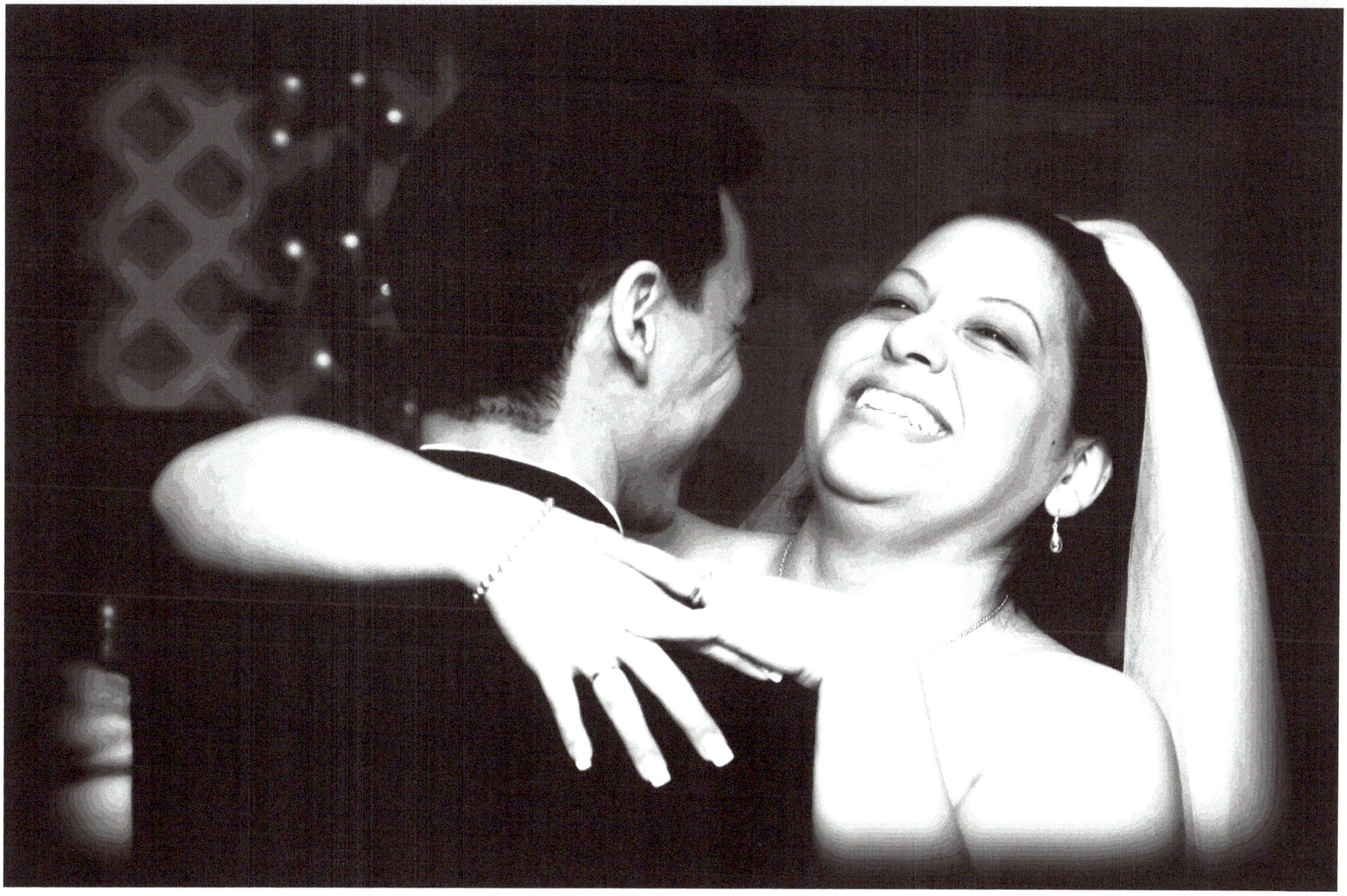

Little ones.....

Little ones growing up and special moments like this do not last forever. That's why it is especially important to preserve your wedding photographs. Make sure your photographs are protected and stored. This is also another reason why it is a good idea to hire a professional to ensure many other shots are taken during the special day besides just of the wedding party.

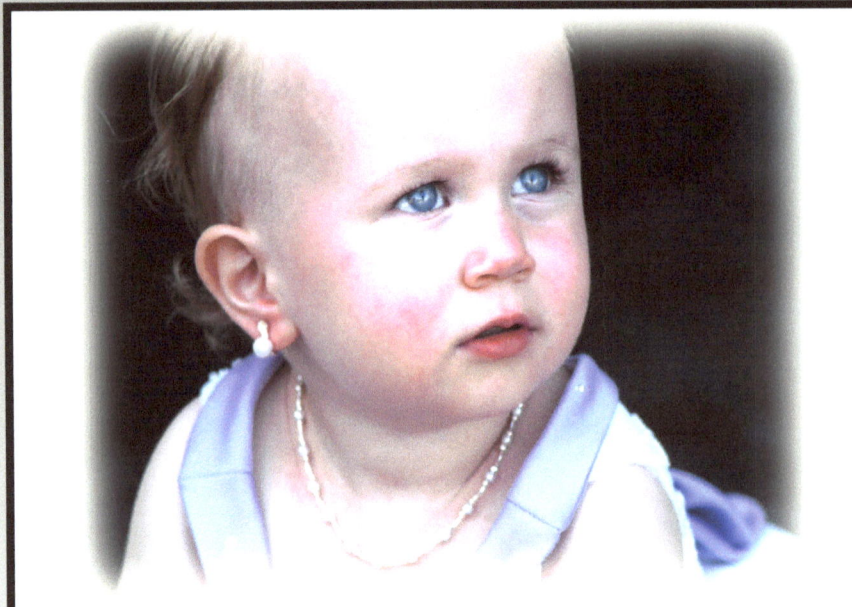

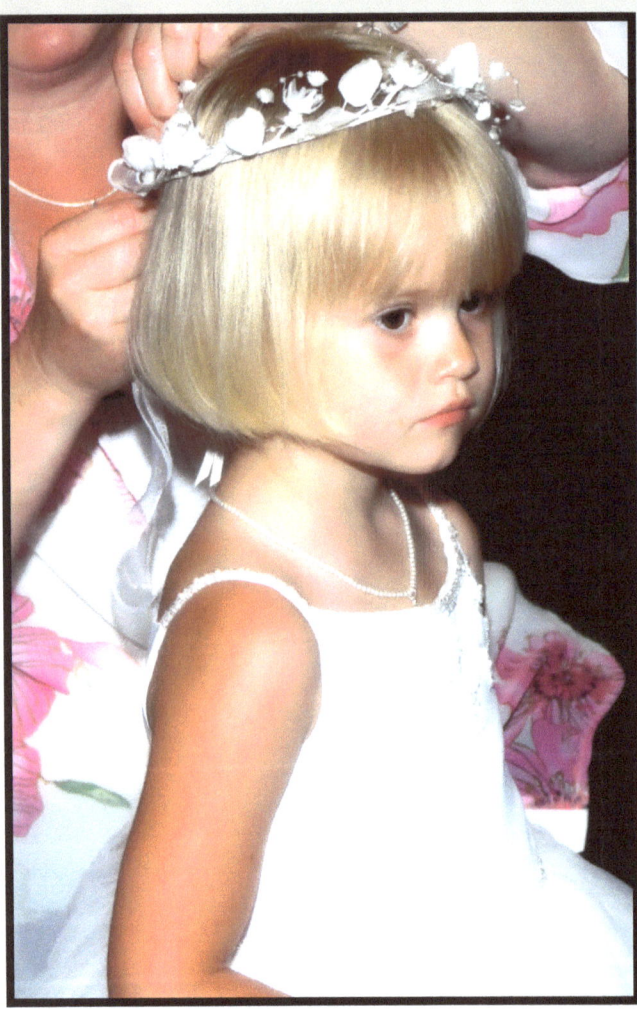

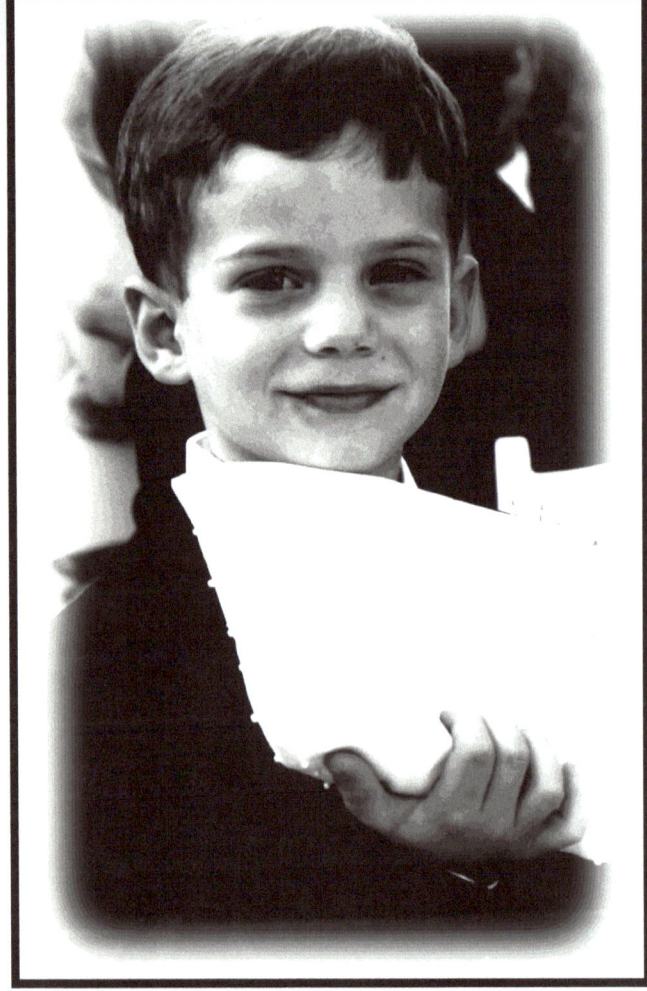

What is the difference between traditional and photojournalism?

Traditional wedding photography can be recognized as formal photographs where people are posed and looking toward the camera "say cheese"! Traditional is characterized by lots of direction, involvement and control from the photographer.

Photojournalism is telling a story with photos. In wedding photography, photojournalism has come to be known as documentary photos of wedding-day events as they happen, with no involvement, direction or control from the photographer. A true photojournalistic photographer will capture a moment as it happens, without orchestrating it, getting in the way, or interrupting the natural process of the wedding. Their goal is to have the least amount of influence possible on your wedding day. It is not their day; it is yours.....yet, still creating the best photos possible is our intention.

We are hybrid style photographers. We shoot an average of 95% photojournalism and 5% traditional. The only time we are in your face is during the formally posed photographs. The rest of the time we capture everything as it happens throughout the day (a true documentary), you will not know we are there! We maneuver unnoticed throughout the day while capturing the brilliance of the special moment. We are true photojournalists....there are no manipulations or interruptions of the special day.

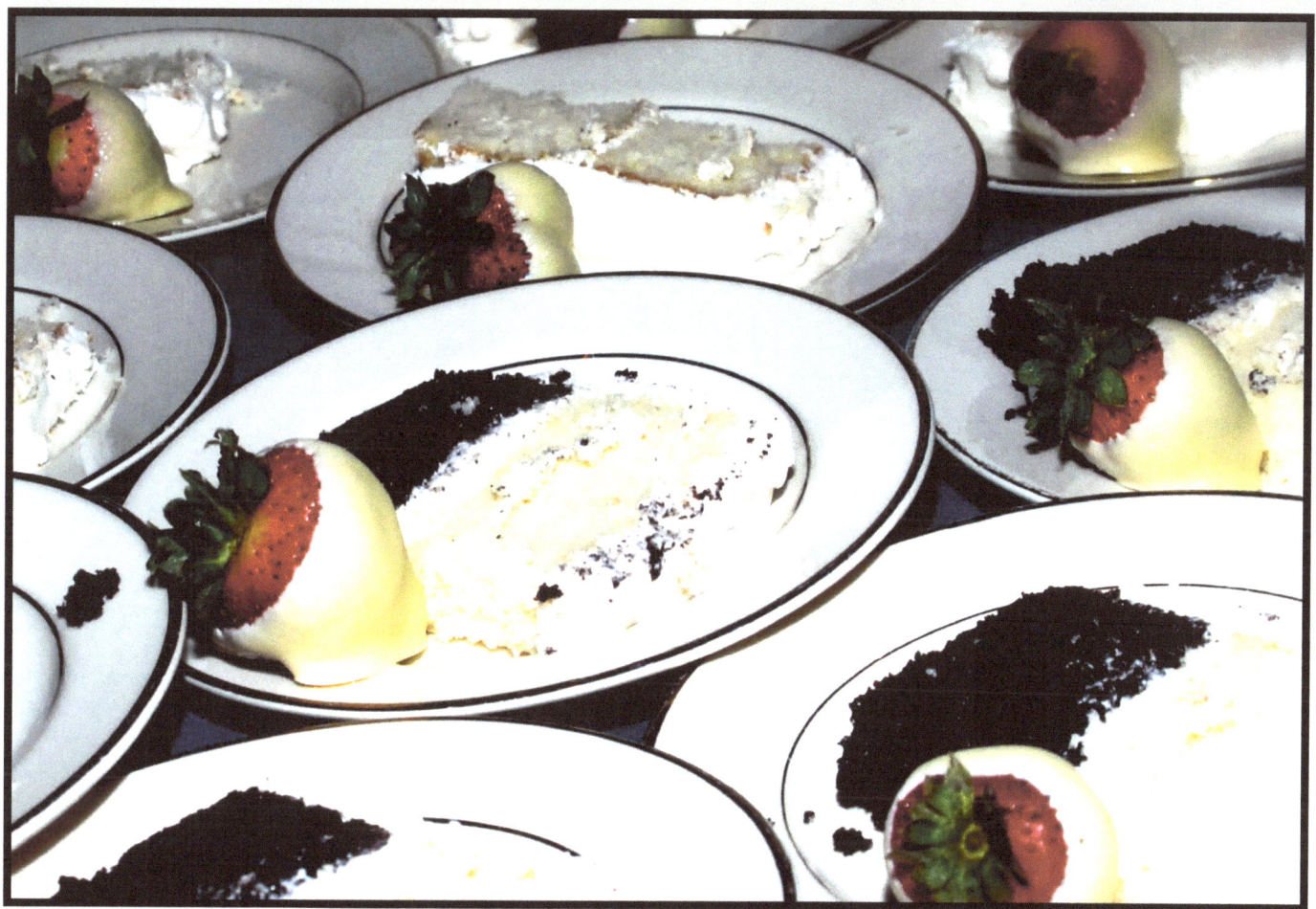

You may not have time to appreciate fine details of this photography when you look at it, but a photograph like this could be right out of a magazine, making a unique addition to your wedding album.

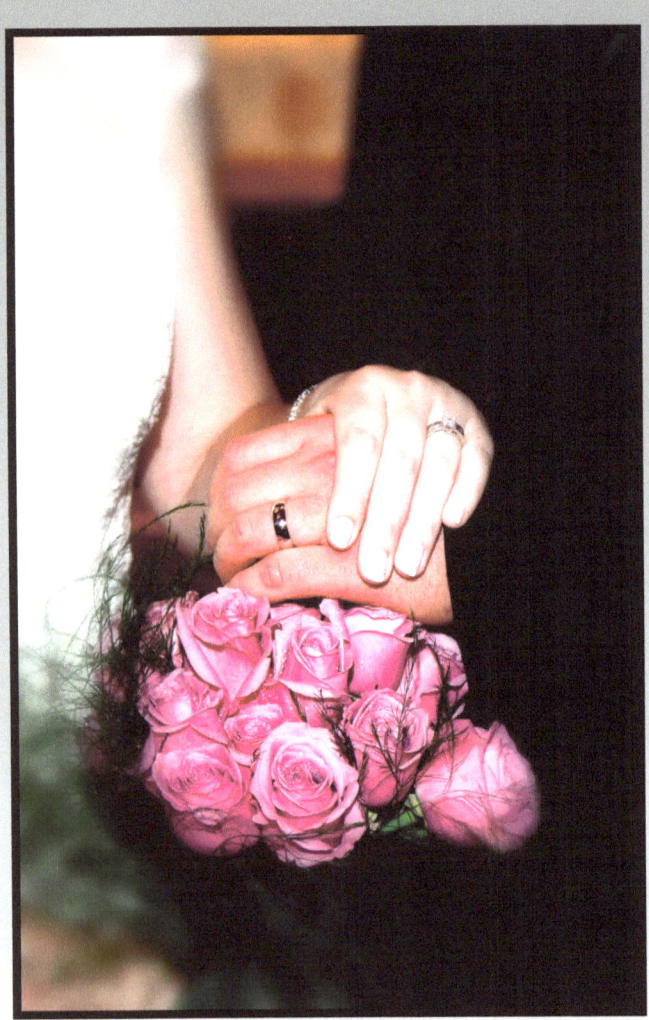

The story is not always told by people's faces

Although wedding photography predominantly shows faces, interesting images reveal themselves in other situations as well. Details such as the bride's shoes, rings, bouquets, etc. convey some of the emotions of the day. Mixed with all of the other photographs, these add to the story of your wedding.

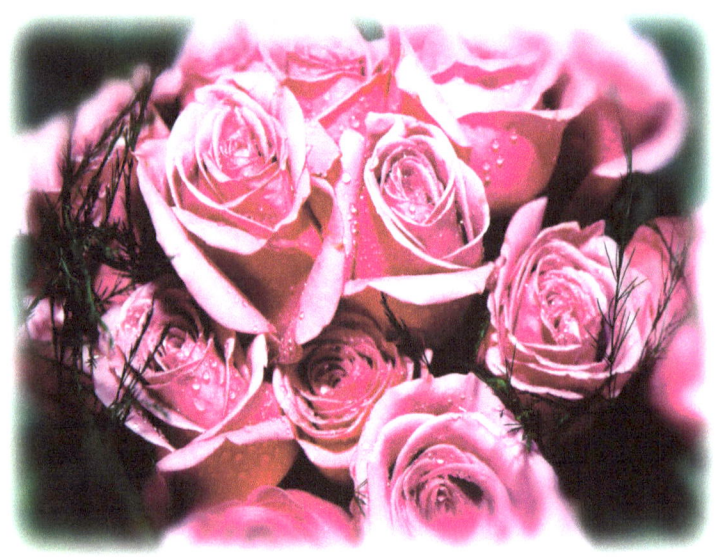

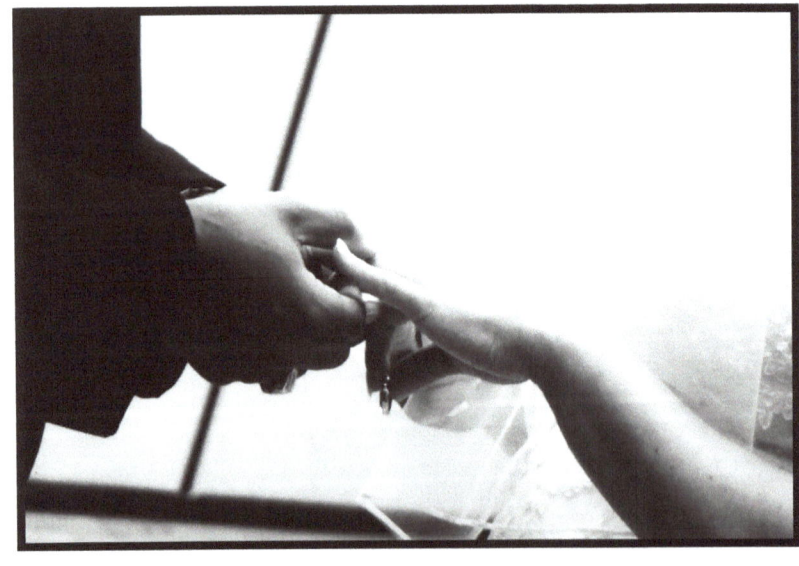

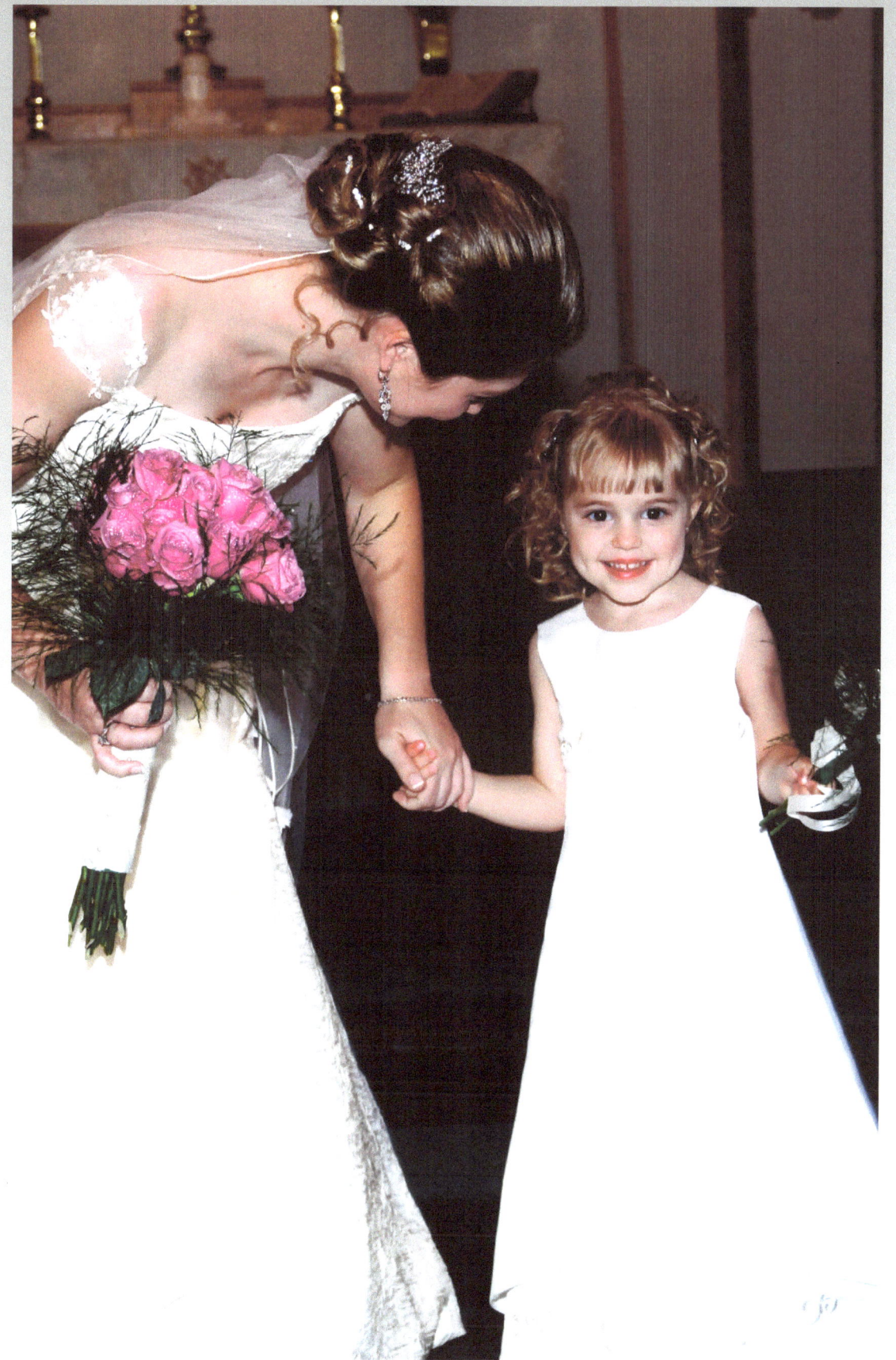

*We even make the smallest members of the wedding party feel at ease! *

What happens after the wedding?

After we leave the reception site and pack up our equipment, we will go home and grab a refreshing drink and load the images on our computer. Once we load the images, we make three copies of your digitally mastered photographs; one copy will be stored on a backup external hard drive that is stored in a fireproof safe. One copy will remain the untouched raw images and the other will be the photographs that will be edited. During day one through ten, your photographs will be edited carefully and reviewed by us. During the editing process, we work our eye for detail and ensure every photograph has proper brightness, contrast and color. We will even go above and beyond to ensure each photograph is the best it can be by going into detail to ensure the ugly exit signs, light sockets, air vents, etc. are removed from the photographs! Also during the editing process, we pick photographs that work well in black and white and convert them and also add special effects. During a normal eight hour wedding day, you will receive approximately 600-800 photographs. You will receive all photographs in full color and the additional photos that are black and white and special effects are copies of the original colored photos. During days ten through fourteen, the photos go in post production, our favorites are added to our website, your photos are burned on a photo DVD (digital negatives), your complementary DVD documentary slideshow is created, and all digital files are backed up on our external hard drive and stored in our fireproof safe. On day fifteen, your photographs will be ready for shipment!

What is the DVD documentary slideshow?

This is the absolute best way to view your wedding day photographs, as it is, a true documentary! Imagine watching a DVD movie of all your wedding photographs from start to finish with background music from your wedding day! You can have your family and friends over, sit in front of the TV and re-live your special moments! The DVD slideshow is completely complementary with all of our packages as a special gift from us to you!

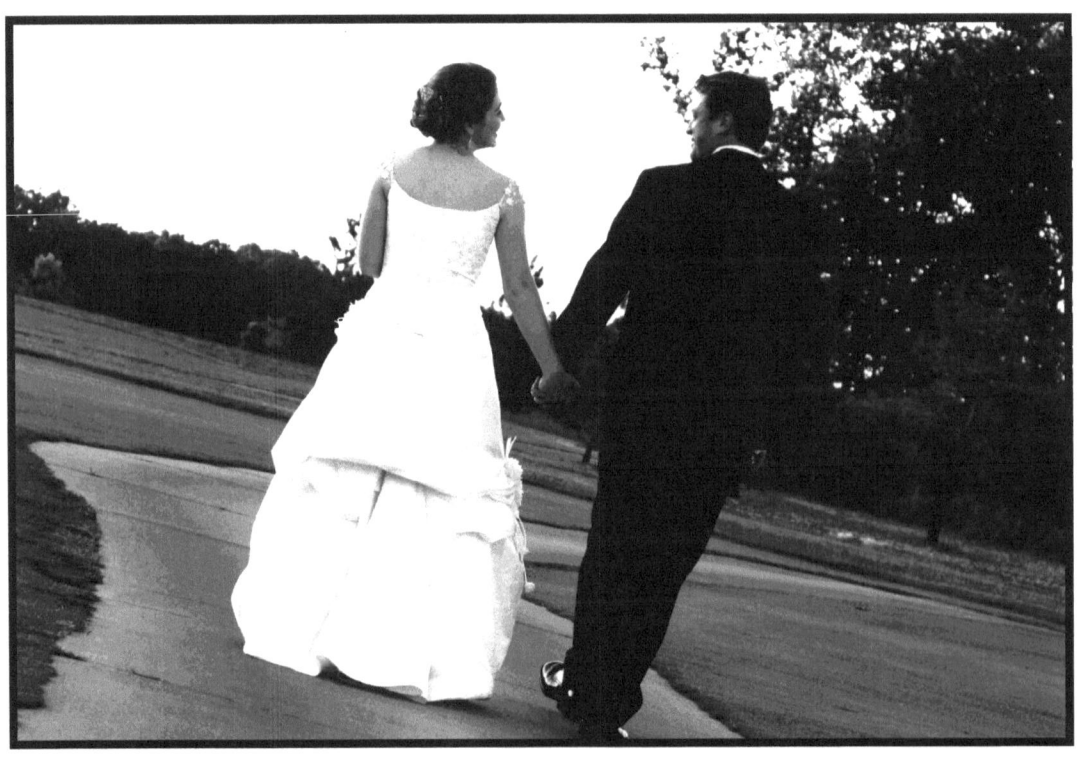

Ask the photographers

We understand that it is very difficult to plan a wedding and sometimes people just only choose what they have seen at other weddings or what they see when they walk into a boutique for the first time. Each wedding should be personalized and have that wow factor for their guests, as well as for you! We want to offer our collective knowledge to you at no extra costs so your wedding is as perfect as it can be, and from a photographer's point of view, the most picturesque as possible. We have been photographing weddings since 1994 and have seen many different colors, locations, styles, traditions, etc. We have seen what works, what does not work, what looks good in photographs, etc. If you are stumped on your colors, location, etc. please let us know and we will be happy to assist!

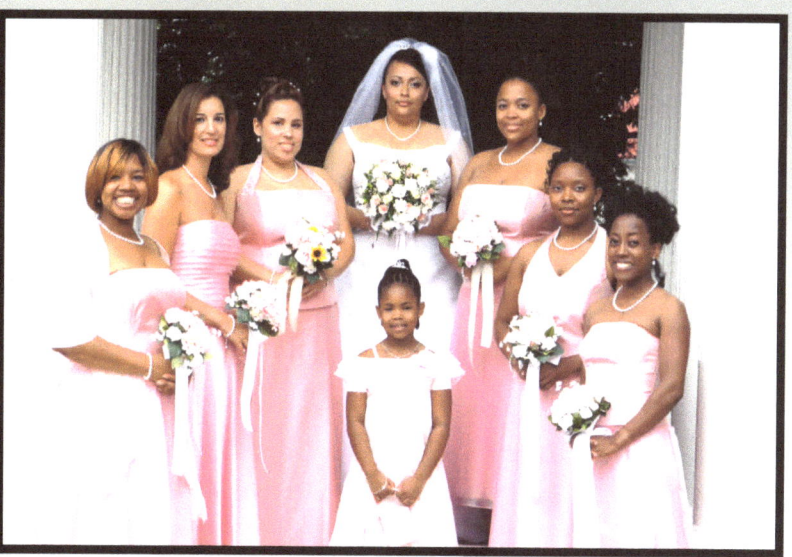

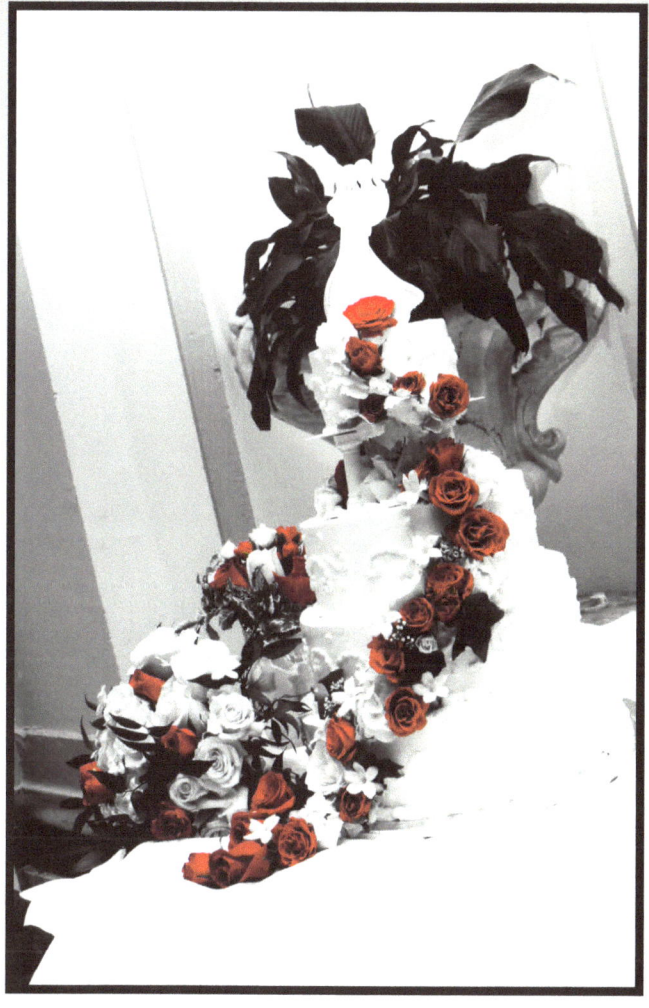

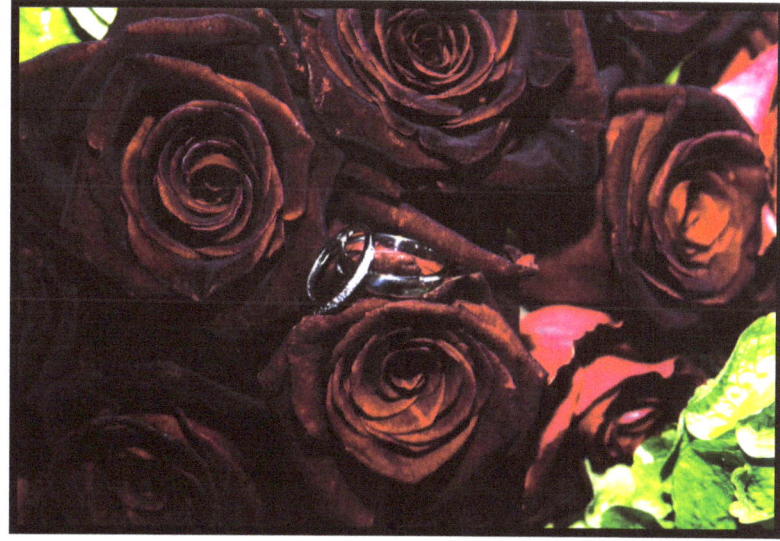

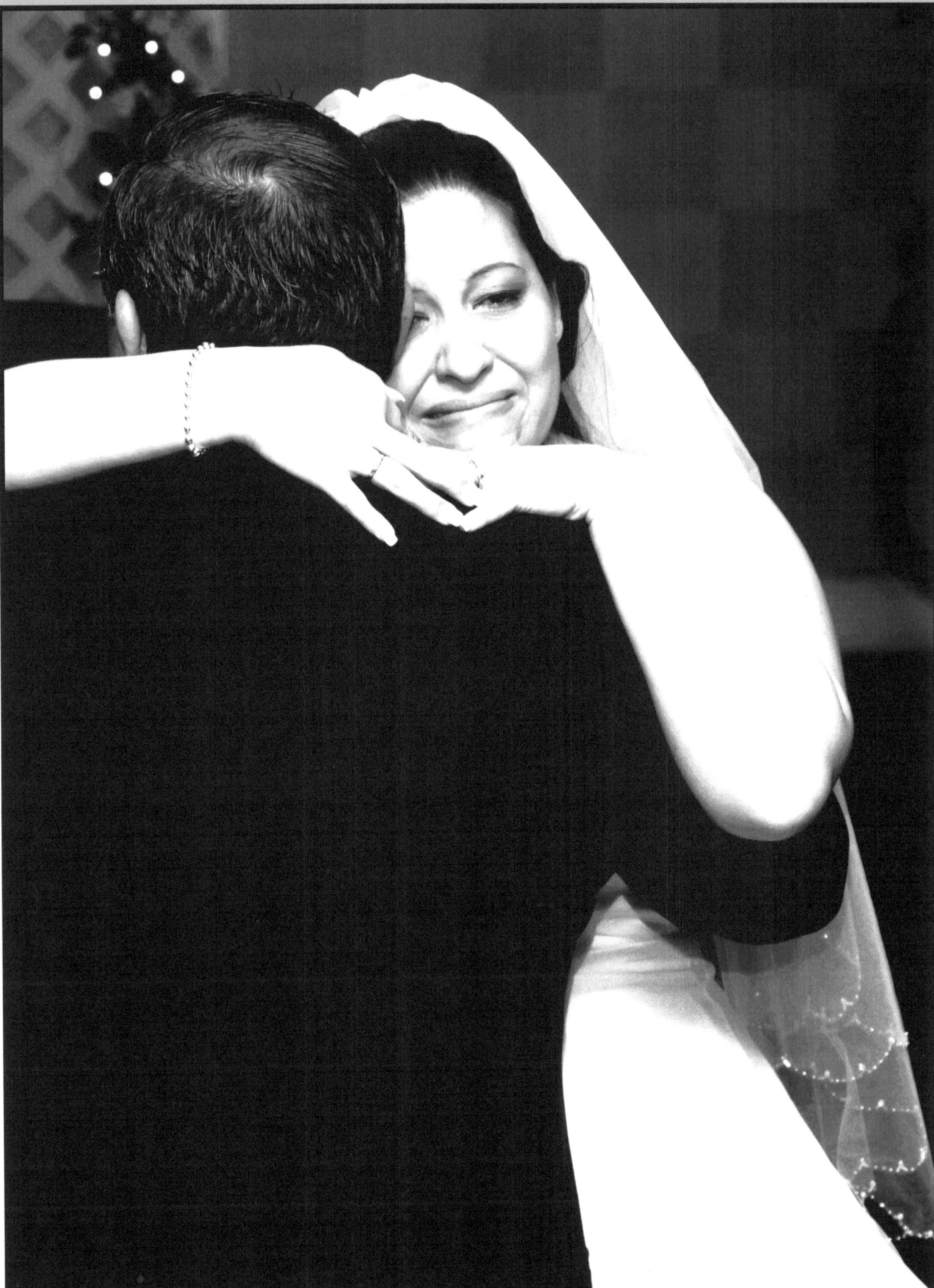

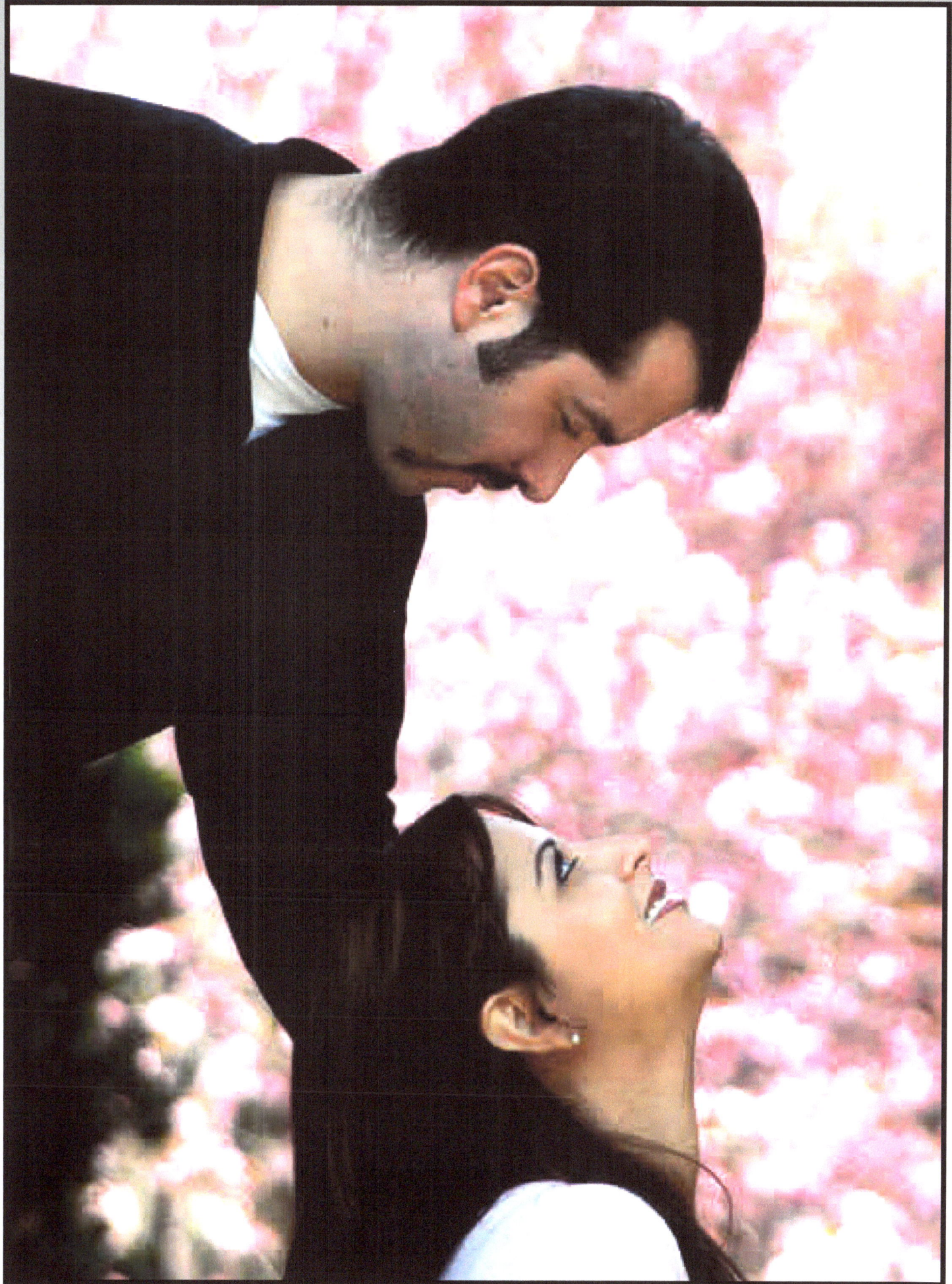

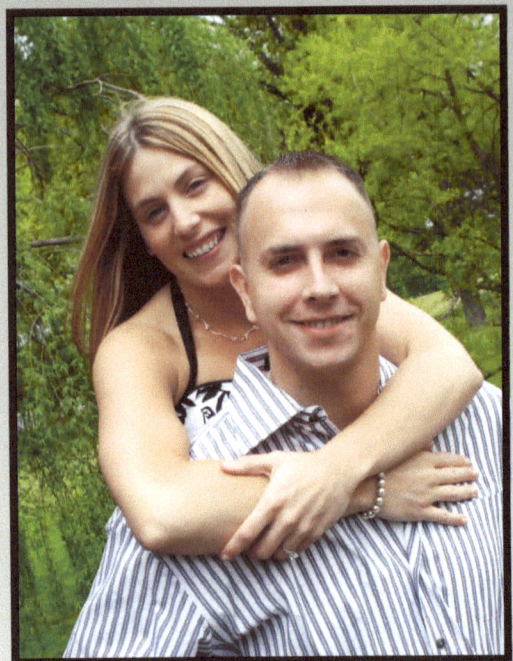
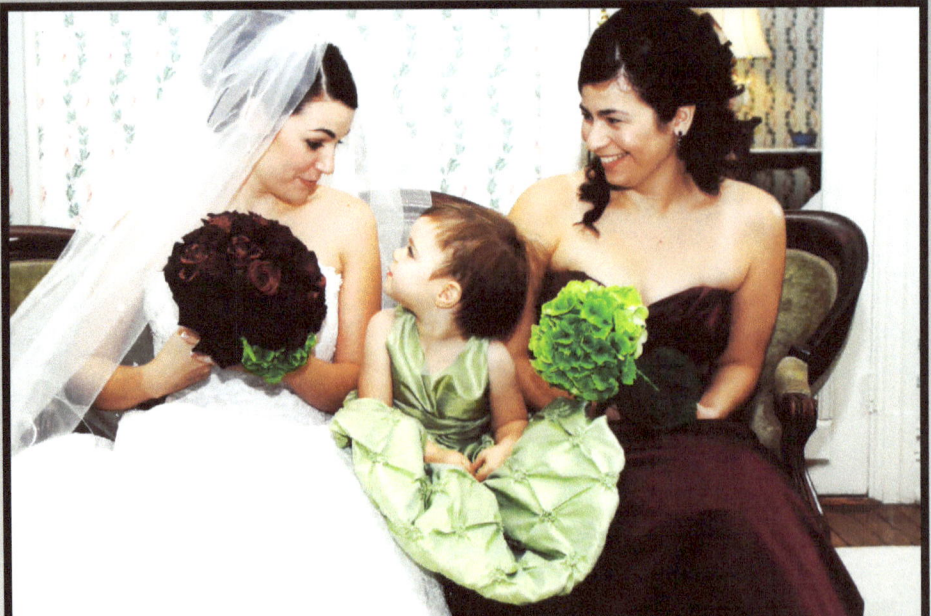
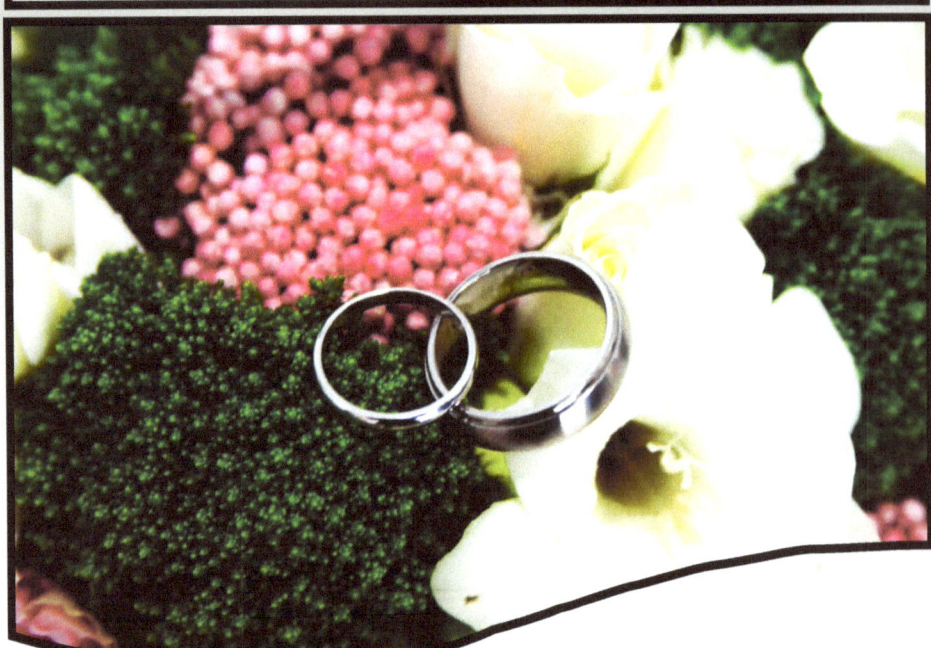
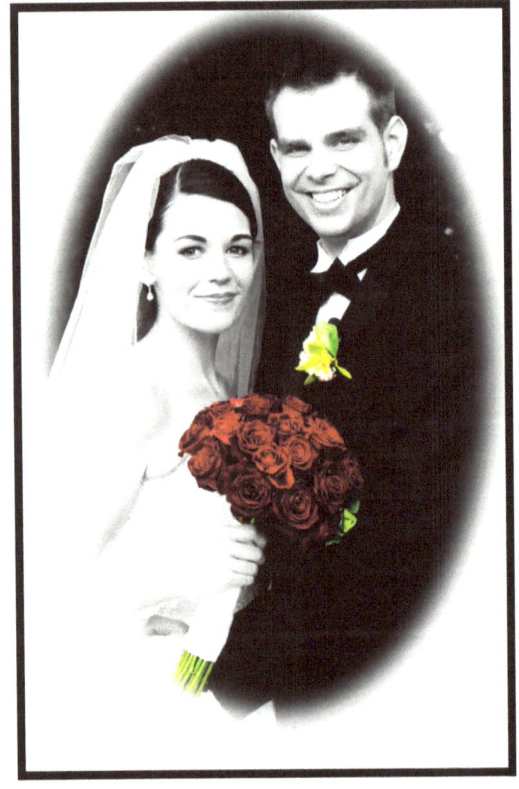
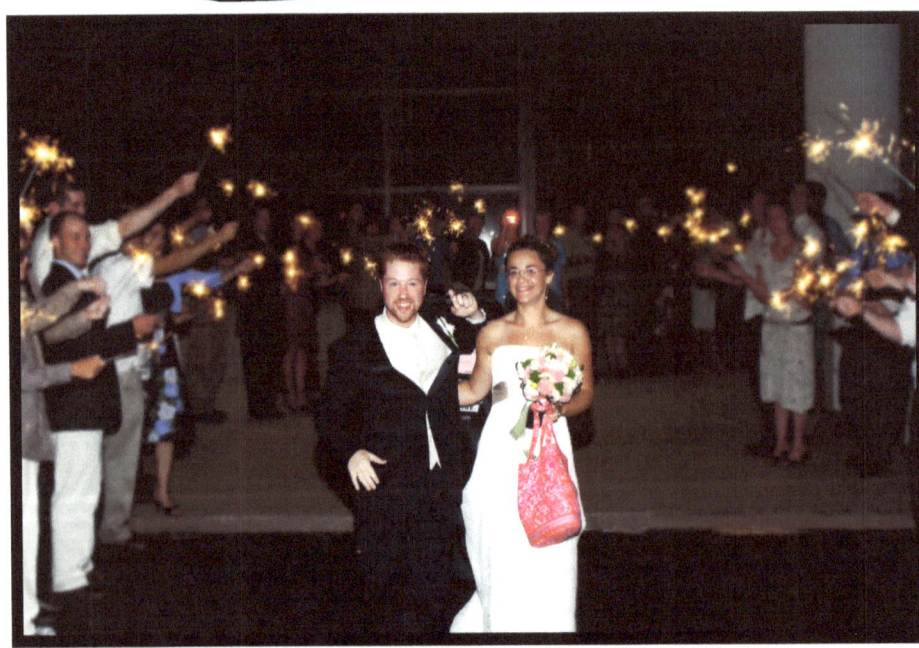

What is copyright?

Remember that your photographs are a work of art and the copyright belongs to the photographer / studio. The COPYRIGHT ACT protects photographers by giving the author of the photograph the right to reproduce your photographs. This includes the right to control the making of copies. It is illegal to copy or reproduce photographs elsewhere without permission. All of our packages include copyright free! That means that we give a letter to our clients stating that we release all copyright of the images taken to our clients and they can reproduce these photographs at will. All we ask is that we can use the photographs for advertising, sampling, etc.

All little ones grow up and special moments like this don't last forever. It is important to take care and preserve your wedding photographs

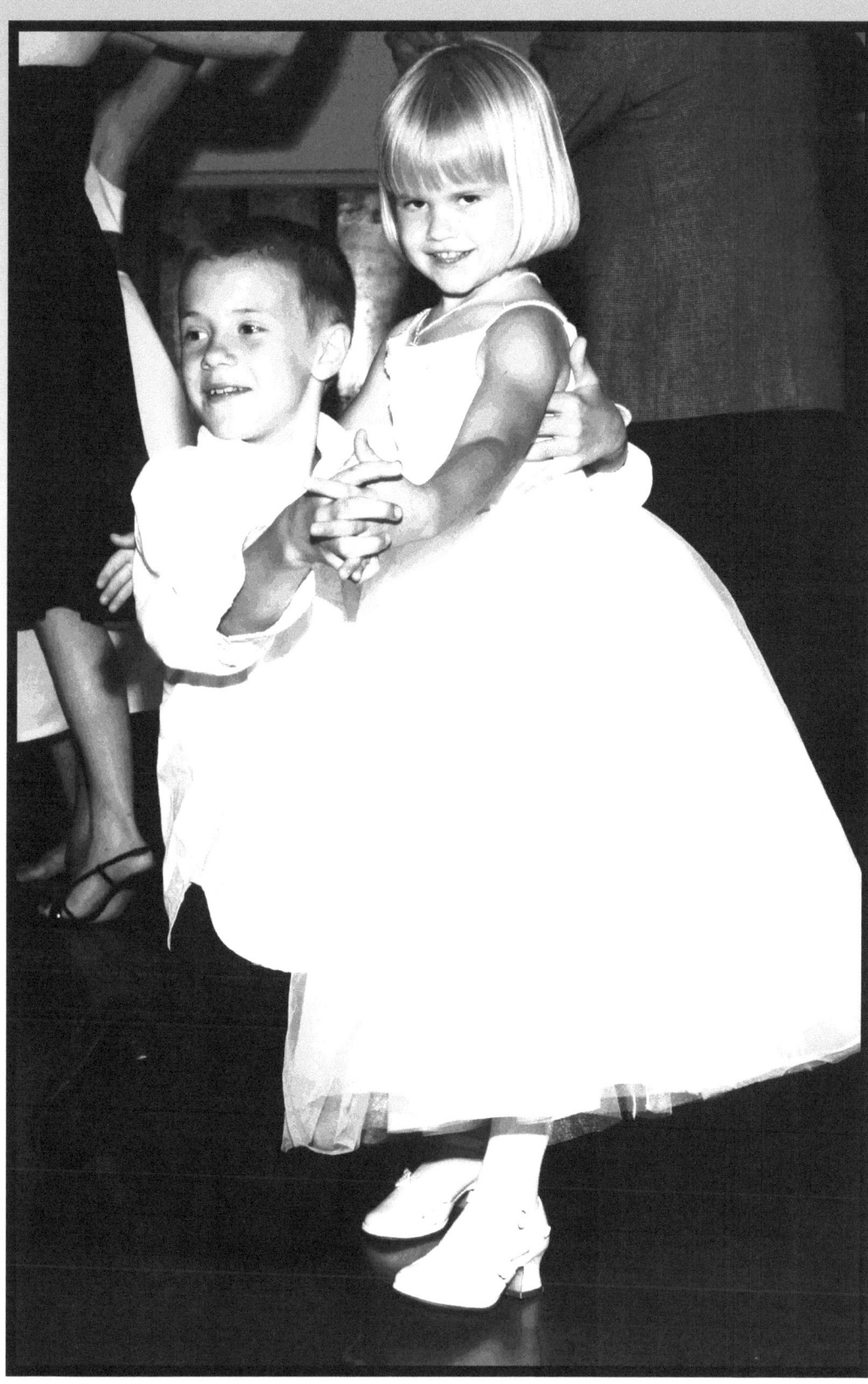

Other colors and B&W

There are a lot of different color enhancements and black and white conversions that can be done to your photographs during the editing process.   When we see a photograph during the editing process that would benefit from these features, we will make a copy and perform the enhancement for you at no additional cost.

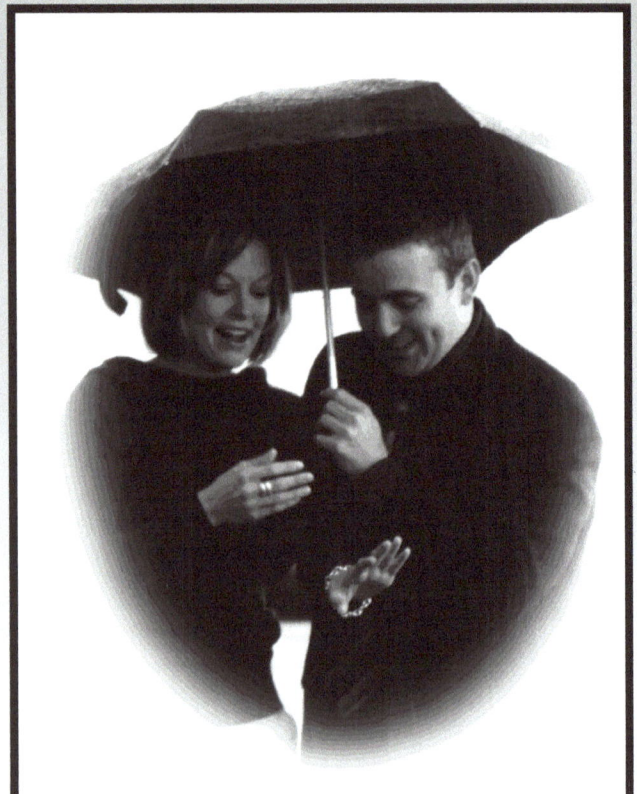

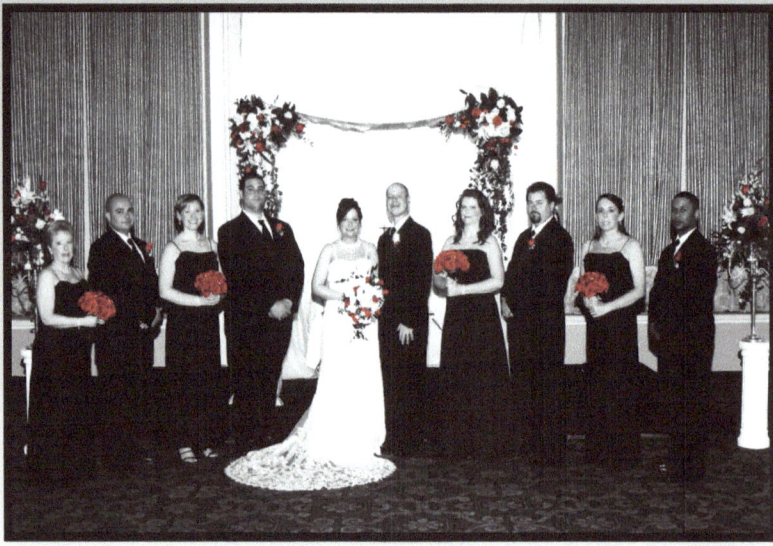

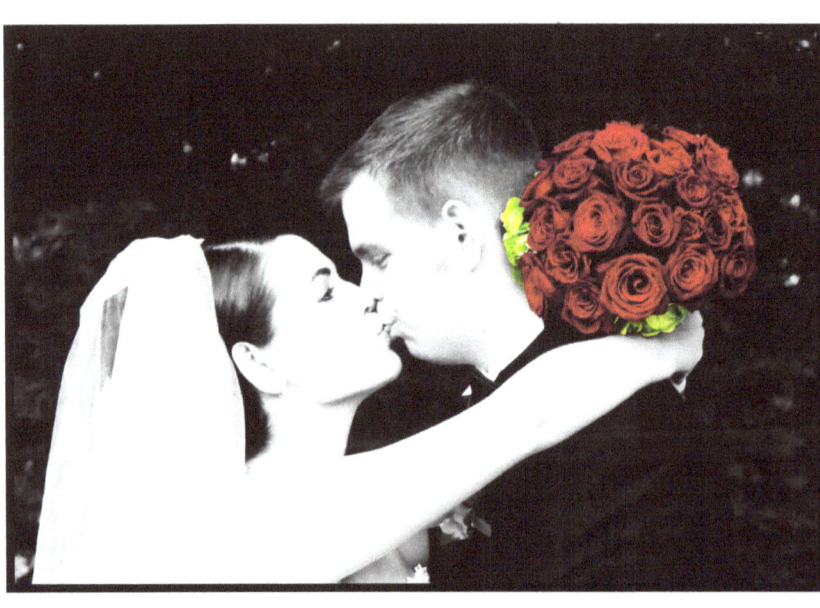

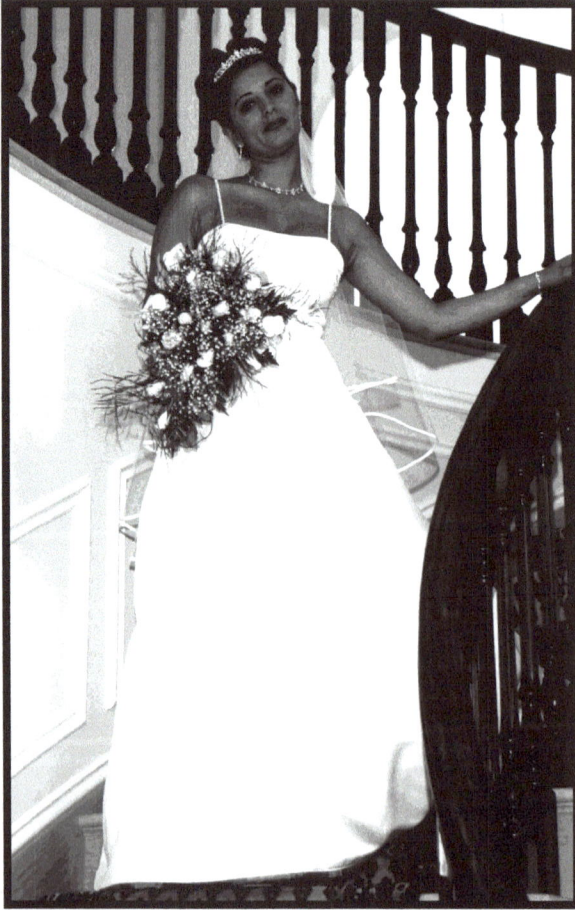

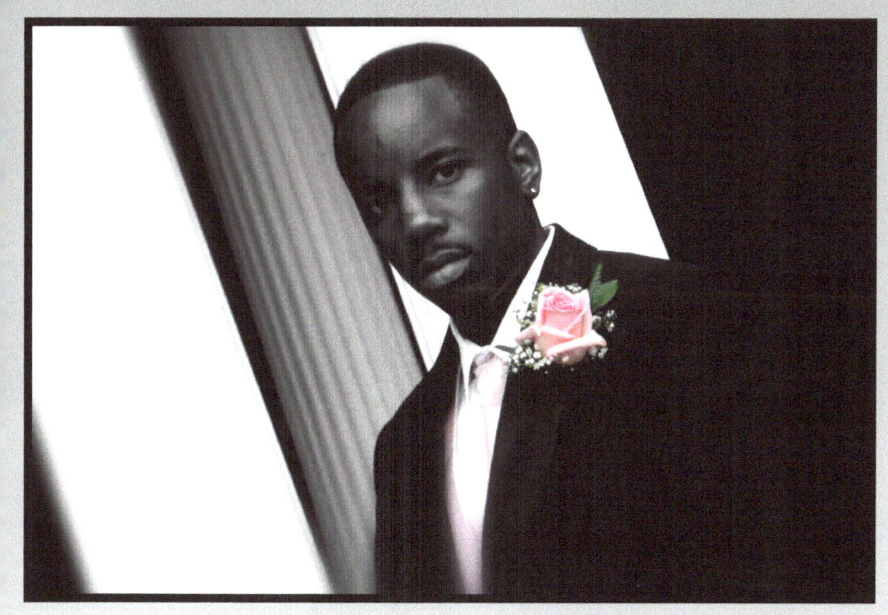

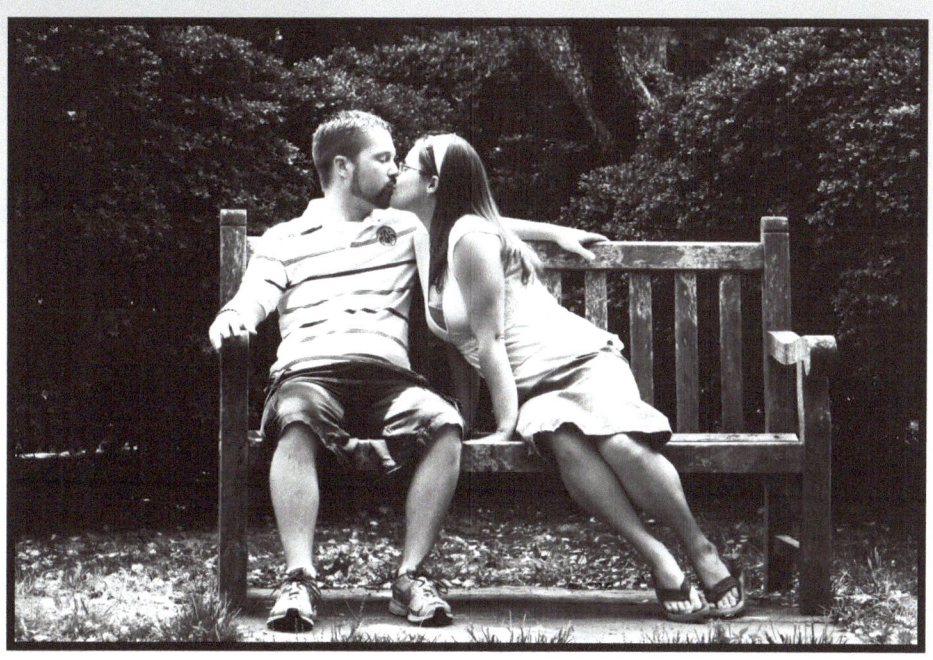

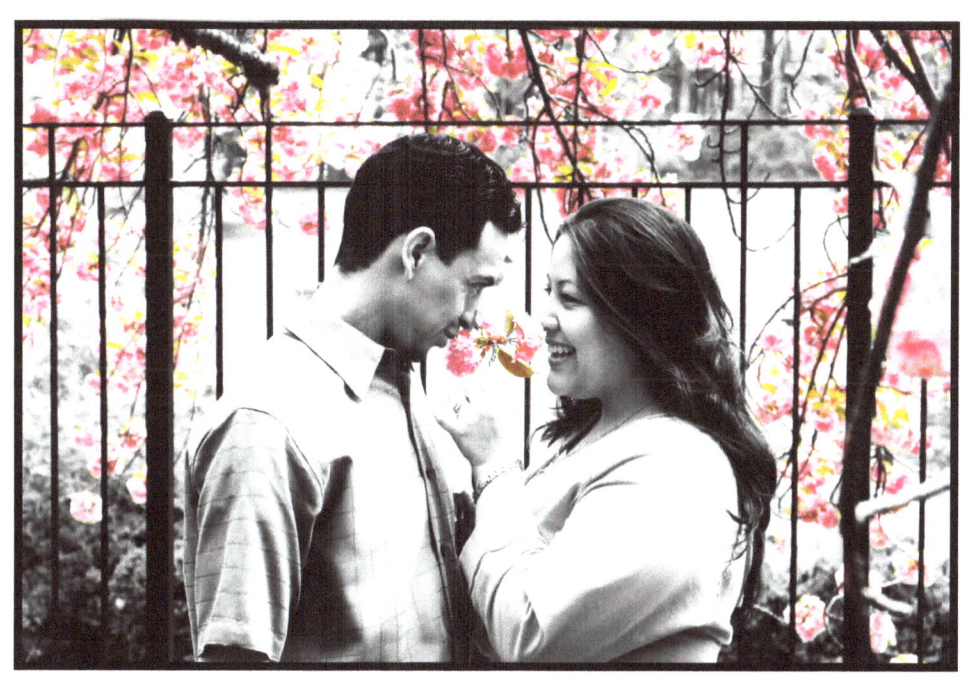

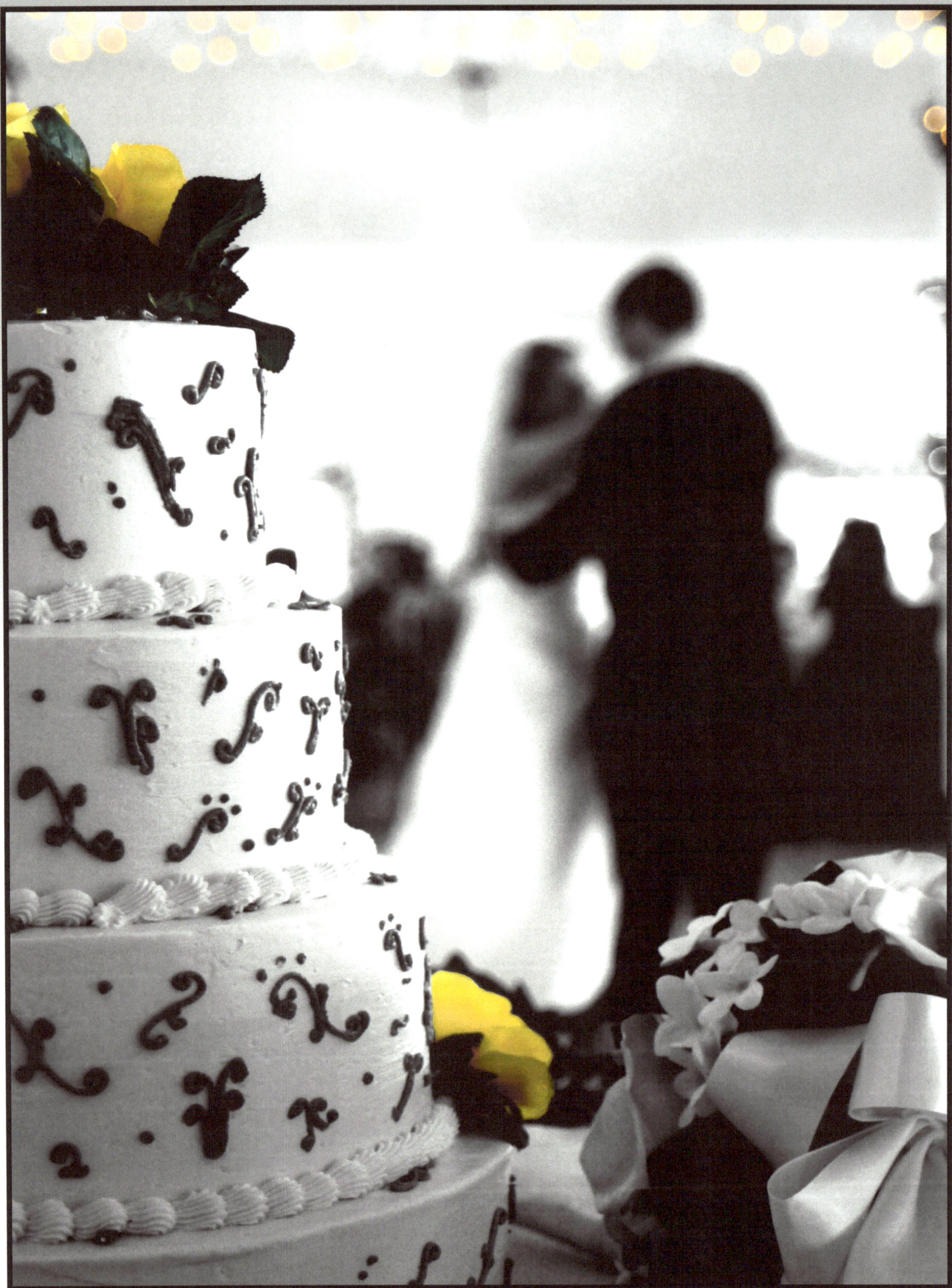

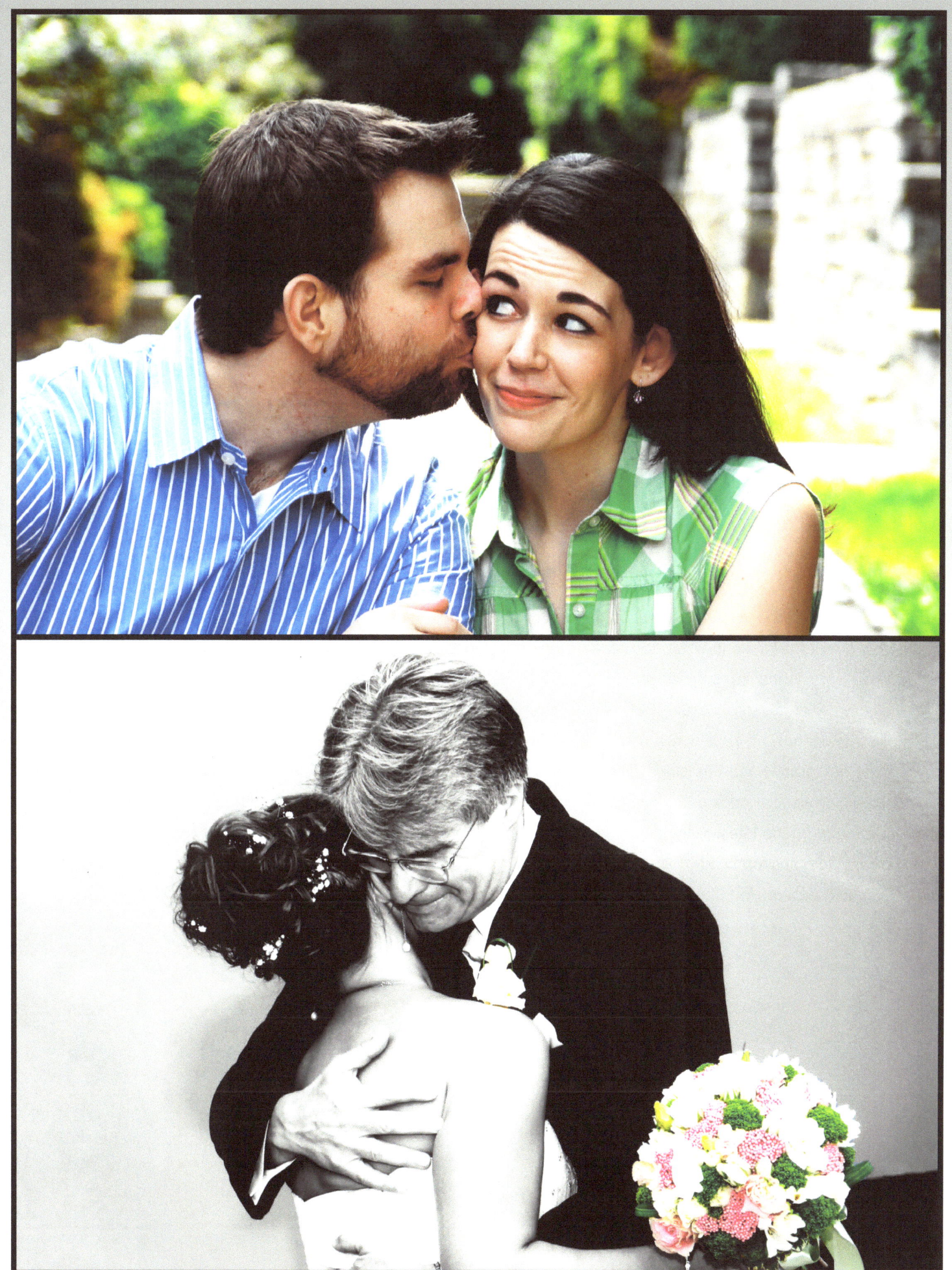

About Pardini Photography and Weddings

Pardini Photography and Weddings is a top recognized successful husband and wife photography team in Montgomery and Frederick County, Maryland. We specialize in wedding, portrait and corporate style photography. We take pride in the impact that we had on our clients since 1994! We work together as a team documenting special, once in a lifetime moments with pure excellence. Kathy takes pride in the connection she establishes with our clients when conducting poses while Craig documents the moment by capturing memories with his impeccable eye and intuition! During times when formal posing is not necessary, Kathy will take photographs so that all angles are captured. By having a male and female photography team, you will get the view of your wedding from both a female and male prospective. Craig and Kathy maneuver unnoticed throughout the day while capturing the brilliance of the special moment. We are true photojournalists....there are no manipulations or interruptions of the special day. Craig and Kathy are both skilled in the latest Adobe Photoshop professional photography editing software and are members of The National Association of Photoshop Professionals.

Craig holds the prestigious Masters of Fine Arts Degree in Photography (M.P.R.) and is a certified master professional wedding and portrait photographer. Craig and Kathy are active members in numerous photography organizations such as: Professional Photographers of America, American Image Press, International Freelance Photographers Organization and The National Association of Photoshop Professionals. In 1990, Craig first started his formal studies as a photographer and was offered a teacher's assistant position for that very same photography course the following year. In 1993, Craig was offered a full scholarship to Brooks College to further his photography and graphics studies. In 1994, Craig established Pardini Images and started photographing weddings professionally. Craig's first wedding was a referral from his photography professor in 1994. Between 1994 and 1999, Craig photographed many different weddings and formal events independently. In 1999, Craig married his soul mate Kathy Ireland and shortly thereafter, Pardini Images changed to Pardini Photography and Weddings. Since Y2K, the team of Craig and Kathy made many differences in people's lives by documenting special once in a lifetime moments with excellence! Craig and Kathy are always continuing to add to their knowledge on the latest cutting edge photography technology. Craig frequently attends photography seminars and Photography / Photoshop continuing educational courses. In late 2008, Craig started instructing a photography class for individuals with autism. In 2009, Craig was inducted into the IFPO Photographers Hall of Fame.

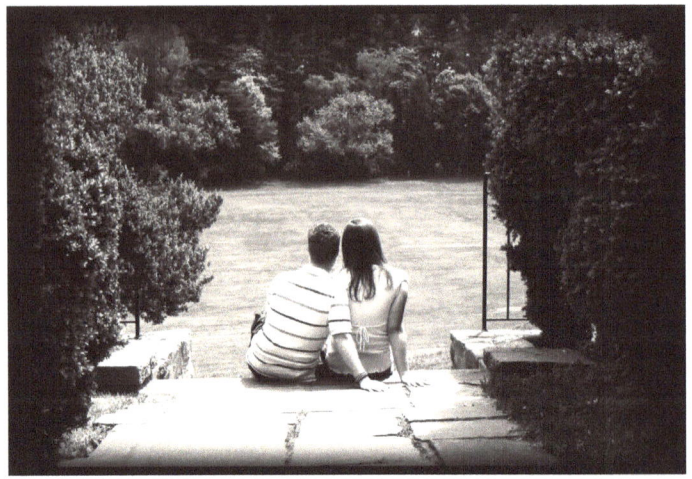 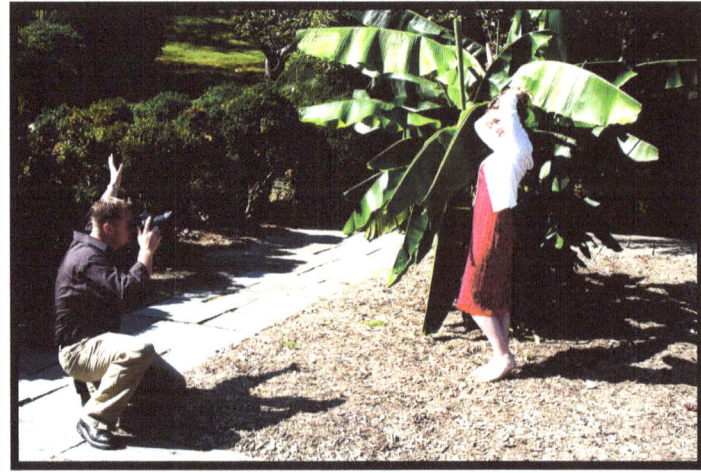

Photography is the art of painting with light, but to us, the real art is getting to know people and capturing incredible photographs of the most special moments in their lives.

Our mission is that your experience will be like having at your side an old, trusted family friend who just happens to be a exceptional photographer that will put you completely at ease.

Our goal is that the photographs we capture, will take your breath away. You will brush back tears by reliving the memories through these photographs that will be passed around the family room for generations to come.

From the very beginning it has been very clear to us, we are not in the business, focusing on business; we are in the people business, focusing on photography!

We use top of the line state-of-the-art technology. As certified professionals, we will use whatever camera is most appropriate for what is being photographed. Do not worry, we have plenty of backup equipment! That is one of the main benefits to hiring an experienced professional photographer. Our state-of-the-art digital technology allows us to offer you more convenient proofing / viewing and editing methods.

We prefer a style that emphasizes the personality and expression of the subjects. Human photography is very challenging, and you need to work with a personality that is upbeat, lively, and sensitive. High end models get paid top dollar because they know how to provide the expressions that sell products and services. The best technique and print quality, however, cannot guarantee a great expression. Since many people are shy in front of a camera, a photographer's skill at establishing a rapport with the subject is extremely crucial and that is what we do! Subjects need to participate when photographed by relaxing and having fun!

Why do we offer excellent services? Because we love what we do. This is not our fulltime job, we do not have to do this at all, we just enjoy what we do and pass that on to you!

What to expect after your event?: the very same day of your event, we make three backup copies of your digitally mastered photographs, one copy of which goes on our backup hard drive and stored in a fireproof safe (to preserve for a lifetime). Your photographs will then be precisely edited, carefully reviewed by us and added to our website for you and your family to view conveniently. Two weeks (or sooner) after your event takes place, your package will be complete and ready for you to enjoy! We are good friends with all of our past clients. The connection that we establish during the planning process, engagement session and the weddings, brings us close for many years to come. That is why we succeed in what we do!

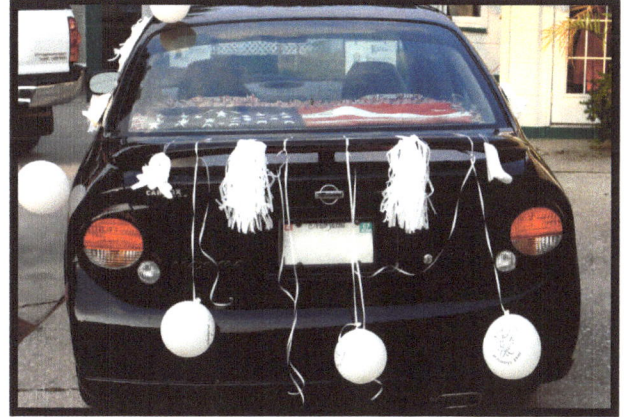

Referrals

When deciding on your wedding day photographer, it is always a good idea to ask for referrals or testimonials..... The ones below are a few of our favorites.....

Amy and Matt (Wedding): Craig and Kathy have once again hit it out of park! Matt and I were over the moon about our engagement photos and now we are in awe of the 3 wedding albums we have full of beautiful portraits and memories that we will never forget. Craig and Kathy captured the excitement and love of our special day and now we have wonderful keepsakes that we can share with our friends and family. They also included a wonderful DVD slideshow full of perfect music to accompany every photo... we were both in tears! Thank you so much Craig and Kathy. You are a true dream team and I know that you will be a part of our lives for a long time and will be there to help us capture even more memories to come! Much Love and Thanks <3

Amy and Matt (Engagement): Craig and Kathy are a cool, young couple who we immediately bonded with during our engagement photo session! It's so important to feel comfortable with the people who are going to be documenting the most important day of your life, and Craig and Kathy are definitely a PERFECT MATCH! We are pleased as punch with how wonderful our engagement photos turned out and can't wait until our wedding day! They combine the most current technologies with old school charm and produce the most wonderful photos. I recommend them highly! :D

Dave: Here is a testimonial from a past "Father of the Bride", to all future "Father of the Bride's". Your Daughter's wedding day is the most important day for her, and you will want that day to be special. There are many things when planning that day that you will stress over, because like all Father's, you will want your Daughter's wedding day to be a wonderful memory that will last forever. The one thing that I did not stress about was our photographer's, who were Craig & Kathy Pardini. They made the memory of our Daughter's wedding, something that we will cherish forever. When I first met with them, I knew that I had made the right choice, and now I and my family consider them to not only be our dear friends, but members of our family. To Kathy & Craig, I thank you for making this past "Father of the Bride" forever grateful. We love ya!

Angela and Mark (Wedding): We are so happy with our wedding pictures! Kathy and Craig are wonderful! The pictures are just beautiful. They were able to capture the beauty of our day in every aspect of the word. On top of the amazing pictures they did an incredible DVD for us. It started from the beginning of the day all the way to us leaving the reception. The music was paired perfectly with the photographs. We would recommend Kathy and Craig whole heartedly to anyone getting married!

Angela and Mark (Engagement): Craig is an unbelievably talented artist. And I say "artist" instead of photographer, because his photos are indeed works of art. Our engagement pictures were so beautiful. Kathy has that unique ability to capture not just the beauty of the surroundings, but also the beauty of the moment. Craig and Kathy were such a pleasure to work with, and we had so much fun! We are so excited to have them as our photographers for our wedding. After seeing how well the pictures came out for the engagement session, we can't wait to see the wedding pictures. Thanks again Craig and Kathy for capturing the essence of our love so beautifully!

Katy: Craig and Kathy are a young, fresh couple who add up to date technology with the utmost professionalism and personalism. The images they captured for my sister's engagement and wedding are priceless. The Pardini's do not just deliver photos. They truly know how to capture the warmth, love and feelings not only with the bride and groom, but the entire family.

Jill and Brian: Craig & Kathy, I could never say enough good things about the two of you. You both have become like family in such a short period of time. I felt so comfortable with the two of you the first time I met with you. The pictures you took of not only our engagement but also our wedding captured the love and excitement of the moment. The talent you posses is amazing. I would and have recommended you to everyone and anyone that I know. Everyone was so impressed with all of the photos. You could really tell that you have great pride and enjoyment in what you do. Thank you for everything. I really hope that we get to the chance to work with you again.

Daniel and Kjirstin: We cannot thank you enough for your high degree of professionalism and care on our wedding day combined with exceptional photo quality delivered promptly after. You captured our special day with such detail through your lens to make our memories last a lifetime. I would confidently recommend your services to anyone looking for superior services.

Ask questions

When you interview your photographer, it is good to always ask questions and know the answer that you are looking for to base your decision off of….. Below are just a few questions and how we answer that can help you get started.

How many photographers will be at my wedding? 2 photographers will be present! Craig and Kathy personally photograph all weddings together. This has advantages over a single photographer. Kathy will capture the bridal preparations while Craig meets with the guys. By having a male and female photographer, you will get the view of your wedding from two different perspectives. We both work as discretely as possible to capture all the candid moments that an individual photographer would not necessarily see. During the times of formally posed photographs, Kathy will set up the pose while Craig captures the moment.

How many photographs will I receive on my photo CD/DVD? For a normal 8 hour wedding, we approximately take anywhere between 600 - 900 images. You will receive all the photographs on your photo CD/DVD (digital negatives) in a JPEG format so that you may bring them anywhere you choose for printing.

When will my photographs be ready and what do I expect after my event? The very same day of your event, we make three copies of your digitally mastered photographs; one copy will be stored on a backup external hard drive and stored in a fireproof safe. For the next fourteen days, your photographs will be edited, carefully reviewed by us, and added to our website for you and your family to view. Two weeks after your event takes place, your photo DVD/ CD (digital negatives) will be complete and ready for shipment!

What type of equipment does your company use? We use top of the line, state-of-the-art technology. As certified professionals, we will use whatever camera is most appropriate for what is being photographed. Do not worry; we have plenty of backup equipment! That is one of the main benefits to hiring an experienced professional photographer. Our state-of-the-art digital technology allows us to offer you more convenient proofing / viewing and editing methods. Our current inventory includes the newest Nikon digital cameras.

Can I view examples of your work? Yes, you may view examples online by visiting our online portfolio at _www.pardiniphotography.com_. In addition, if you live close to the Germantown, MD area, we can visit you with our sample albums for viewing in the comfort of your own home or at a local coffee shop, etc. in the area.

Do you have referrals or testimonials? How many do you want? You can view some of our latest testimonials on line at _www.pardiniphotography.com/testimonials_ or we will be happy to send you some.

Why are your prices less than other photographers? Most photographers sub-contract their work out like editing, website work, CD/DVD processing, promotional materials, etc., where we do everything ourselves…..saving us money so we can give the savings to you. From the very beginning, our mission has been very clear….we are not in the business, focusing on business; we are in the people business, focusing on photography….we have fun with what we do!

What if your camera breaks? Every piece of equipment has at least one back-up

Do I get to keep the negatives? Yes! Every package includes a photo CD/DVD (digital negatives)

Consider this

The truth is, great photography often happens because the photographer has "been there, done that." We have been photographing weddings since 1994 and know exactly where to be and when to be there. With our detailed eye and intuition, we are confident that your wedding will be documented the best that it can! For example, if you have a friend or family member or a inexperienced photographer photographing your special once in a lifetime day, he or she may very well miss a lot of very important and special events of your wedding. He or she may be involved in a conversation with another guest, while the bride and groom are cutting the cake. Or he or she may be eating his cake when the bride is tossing her bouquet. The inexperienced novice cannot anticipate a series of events while a professional can and will stay one step ahead of the action. The safest way to insure that you will be completely satisfied with your wedding photographs is to hire a professional. That is why we give 100% dedication at every wedding. We have had many weddings under our belt since 1994 and pass the experience to you in every photograph we take.

We are always flattered when someone looks at a photograph we created and exclaims how lucky we were to be at that place at the right moment. Luck had nothing to do with it. Superior photos are result of experience, hard work and planning. When there is excellence, skill and experience behind the camera and excellence in front of the camera, photography can become art! Unlike studio shots where the photographer has complete control over both sides of the camera, we only control the behind-the-camera part of the artistic partnership. You control what happens before the camera. That includes choices you make about your dress, flowers, hair, make-up, picture locations, your bridal party's outfits and even where you stand.

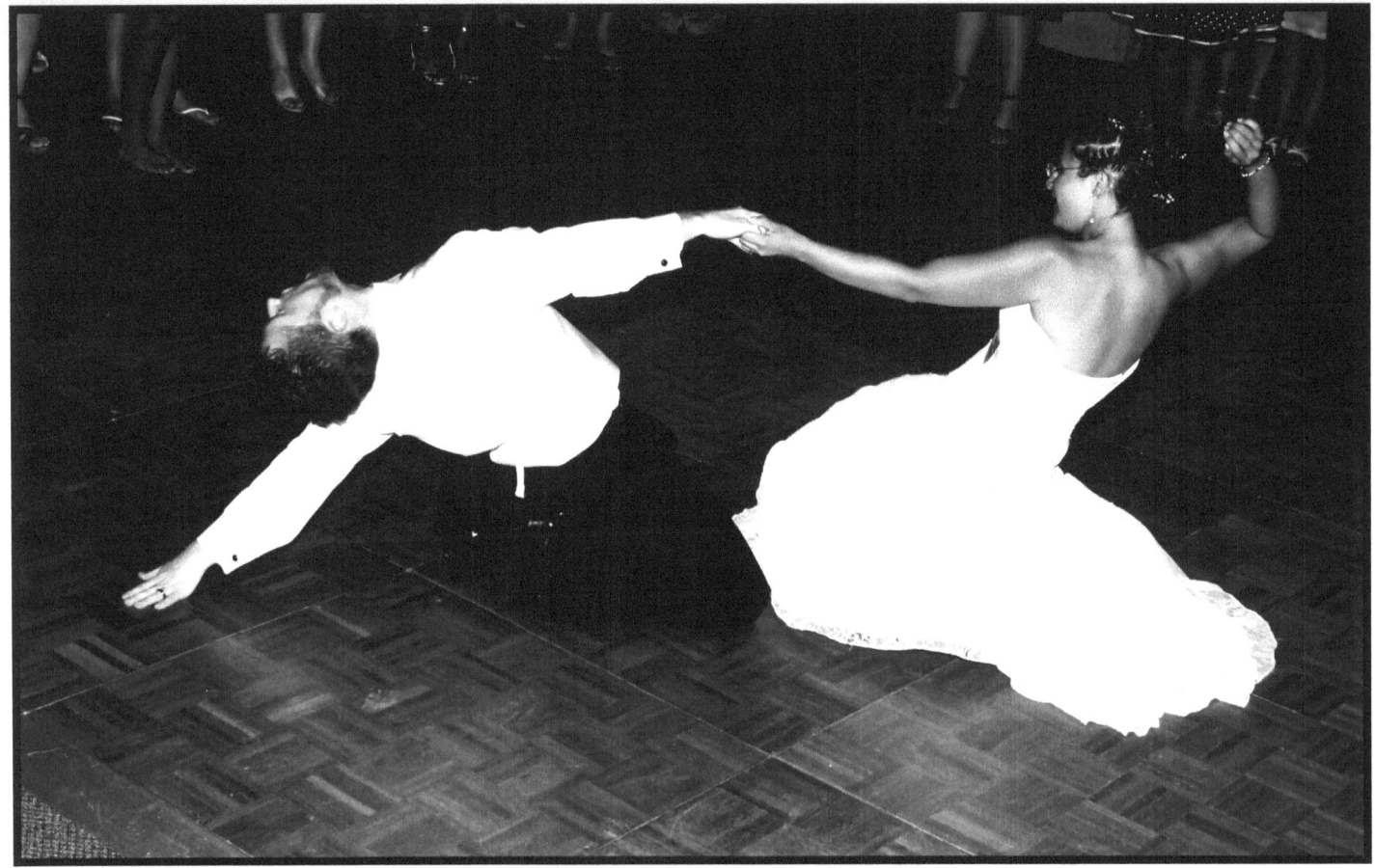

If you plan a special moment together, make sure to let us in on it so we can ensure we can capture the action...

A few final words

It is a long day for photographers. They often begin 2 or more hours before the start of the ceremony and work continuously until the garter and bouquet is tossed. Shooting a wedding often requires 8 or more hours. There are few, if any breaks because they do not want to miss the action. Although it is usually an oversight, brides and their parents sometimes forget to offer the photographer(s) a drink or some food.

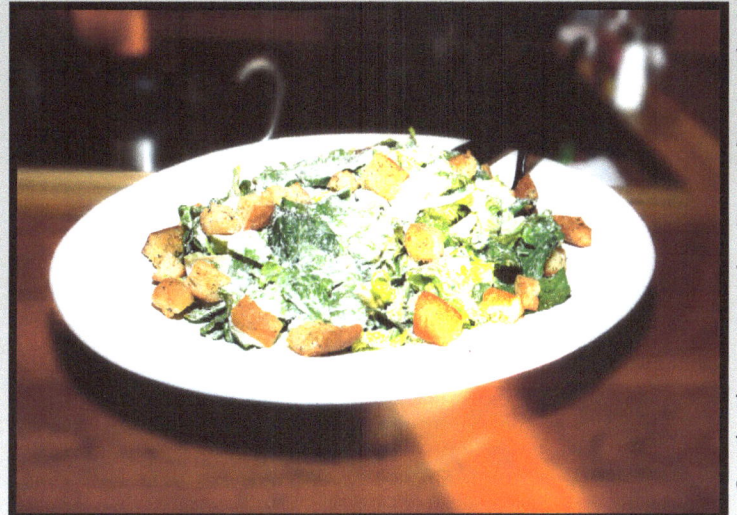

We once shot a wedding during the hottest day of the year in August. The wedding was mostly outdoors and a 10-hour day. During this time, we were not offered a place to sit for a break, (we asked but the room was only set up for an exact number of chairs as were guests) anything to drink or eat. By the end of the day, we were almost ready to pass out. However, since we give the utmost quality and dedication to our clients, not a photograph was missed! It is important to remember that you reap what you sew. While a true professional finds awards in doing the best job possible, no one can do their best after a long day with nothing to eat or drink. Hopefully, this story will help you remember to treat your photographer kindly, so they can take better care of you-photographically.

If you have any questions regarding wedding colors and ceremony/reception locations, please let us know. We have been doing this for a long time and would love to offer advice…..we know what looks best in the photographs!

When having your photograph taken, remember to be yourself! The photos are about you and your day!

It has been great telling you a few tricks of the trade. We hope that this information will help prepare you for what is to come! Please take as much as you can In during your wedding day. Eight hours will seem like 1 hour when the night is over. Your wedding day will be a distant memory 8 years down the road! That is why it is very important to have an exceptional photographer capture your special day in photographs….the photographs will be your memory of a lifetime and something to pass down for generations to come.

We will tell you now and again at your wedding….this is your day and one of the most important days in your lives. We are working for you. If there is a certain photograph you want, please let us know and we will be more than happy to take it for you. The sky is the limit!

We wish you well on your wedding day and look forward to capturing all of your memories with excellence!

Sincerely yours,

Craig & Kathy Pardini

Pardini Photography and Weddings

Your choice in your wedding photographs is among the most important decisions you'll face. Out of everything that is purchased for your wedding, the photographs are the only thing that will keep your memories lasting forever.

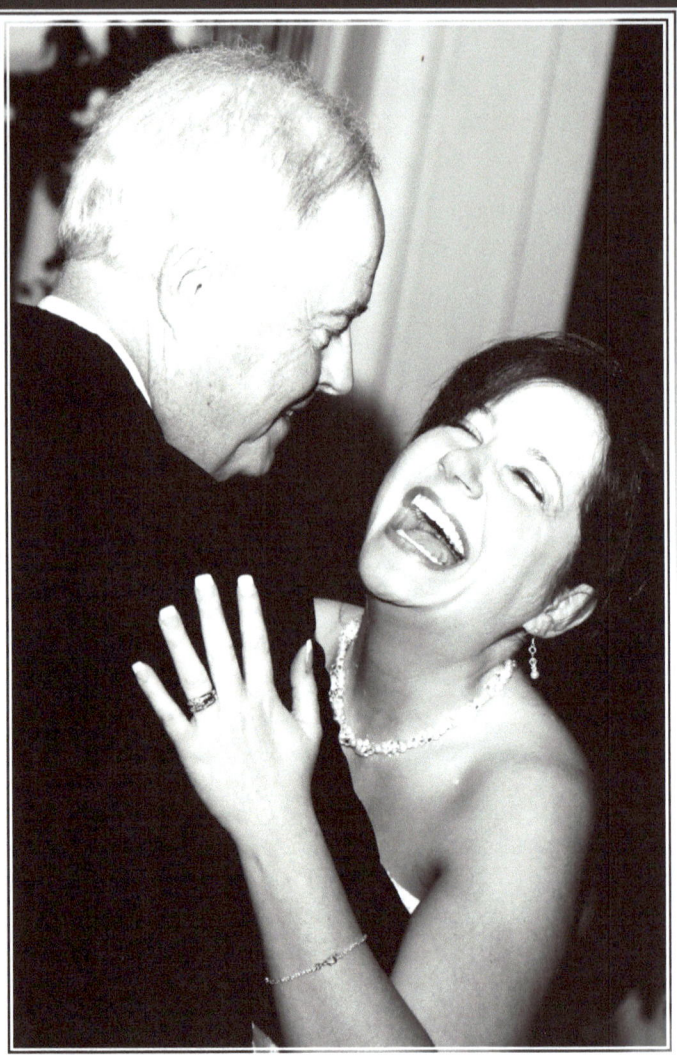

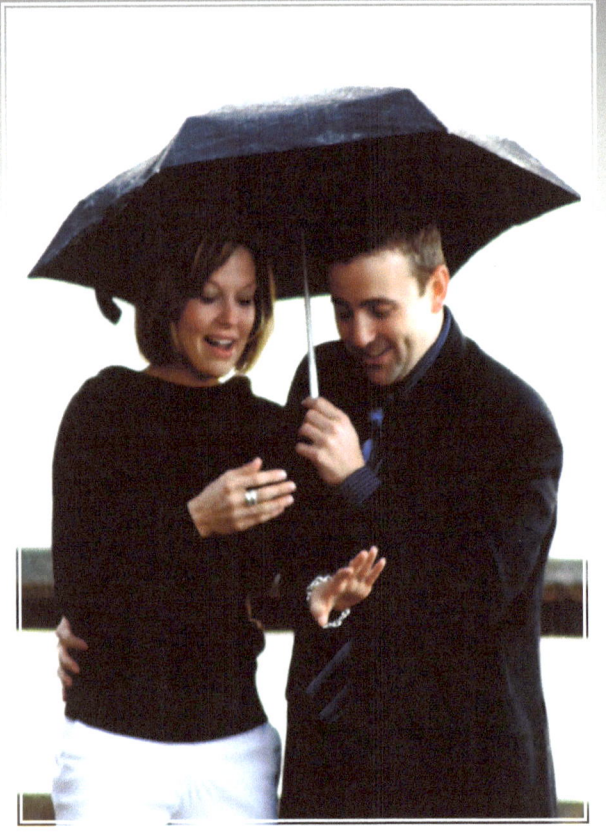

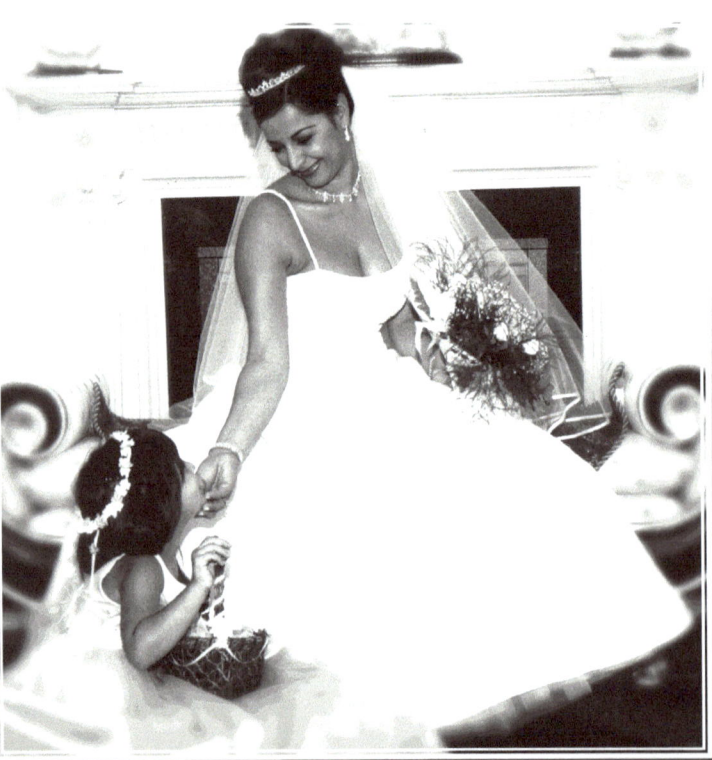

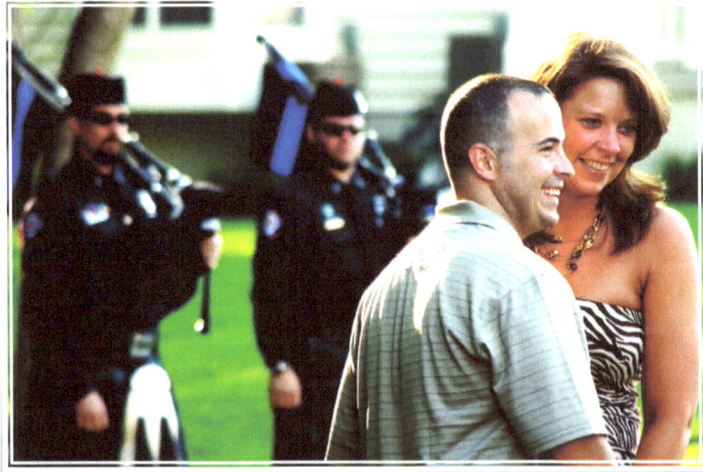

For more information, please visit our website at:
www.pardiniphotography.com

or call us at:

240.426.0098

www.ingramcontent.com/pod-product-compliance
Lightning Source LLC
Chambersburg PA
CBHW050809180526
45159CB00004B/1608